# BEST PRACTICE FOR THE TOEIC® L&R TEST
## –Pre-Intermediate–

## TOEIC® L&R TEST への総合アプローチ
### —Pre-Intermediate—

YOSHIZUKA Hiroshi

Graham Skerritt

JN225937

SEIBIDO

### 音声ファイルのダウンロード／ストリーミング

CD マーク表示がある箇所は、音声を弊社 HP より無料でダウンロード／ストリーミングすることができます。下記 URL の書籍詳細ページに音声ダウンロードアイコンがございますのでそちらから自習用音声としてご活用ください。

https://seibido.co.jp/ad718

**BEST PRACTICE FOR THE TOEIC® L&R TEST**
**―Pre-Intermediate―**

# はしがき

　あなたは何のために英語を学んでいますか？

　卒業に必要な単位を取得するため？就職の際のエントリーシートにTOEICスコアを書かなければならないから？なるほど。でも、英語は学ぶための目的ではなく、コミュニケーションの道具として学ぶことを、常に思い出していただきたいと思います。自然災害は言葉では解決できません。しかし、世界の各地で起こっている、あるいは起こりそうな紛争はこれを解決するのは人のぬくもりを伴った言葉が必要です。あまり大上段に構えても仕方がありませんが、そうしたことに続く人々の直接的な交流は本当に大切です。人々が交流を通じて互いに世界の各地に知人、友人を持てば紛争が起こるのを防ぐことができるのではないでしょうか。大切なのは自分でしっかりとした英語を学ぶ目的を持つことです。これをしっかりと持っていないと英語学習は挫折してしまうかもしれません。

　今世界の4人にひとりが英語を話す時代です。英語はできて当たり前で、政治・ビジネス・文化交流などあらゆる場面で使われています。また、世界の英語話者の4分の3は私たちのようなノンネイティブスピーカー（非英語母語話者）が占めています。ということは、あなたが英語を使う相手はネイティブよりノンネイティブである可能性のほうがはるかに高いのです。ということは様々な発音上の癖やなまりを聞き取れるようにならなければなりません。世界は正にWorld Englishesの時代です。10カ国の人がいたらそのうち最低でも7カ国の人の発言は聞き取れるようになりましょう。10カ国の人がいたらそのうち最低でも7カ国の人に分かってもらえるような発音ができるようになりましょう。

　本書の発刊に当たり、『BEST PRACTICE FOR THE TOEIC L&R TEST』をBasicからAdvancedまでのシリーズ四部作とすることをご提案いただいた㈱成美堂の佐野英一郎氏、引き続き編集に尽力くださった宍戸貢氏、新しく編集メンバーに加わって的確なアドバイスをくださった松本風見氏、丁寧な英文校閲をしてくださったMatthew Miller氏に改めて御礼申し上げます。

2024年秋

著者代表　吉塚　弘

# 本書の構成と使い方

## ■全般：

・全UnitがDining OutやOfficesなどのトピック別の構成になっています。

・各Unitには、Part 1〜Part 7までの全てが収められています。

・各Partの問題は、Unit 1〜Unit 14へと出題頻度と重要度の観点から配置されています。

## ▶Warm up — Dictation Practice：

・リスニングセクション前の耳慣らしです。

・音声は成美堂ホームページ（https://www.seibido.co.jp/ad646）よりダウンロードあるいはスマートフォンやタブレットでストリーミング再生してください。

・日本人にとって聞き取りにくい音の変化を学べるようになっています。聞き取りの際の注意点は、"Points to Dictate"にあります。

・聞き取るだけでなく、自分でも発話できるように繰り返し練習しましょう。

・Unitを追うごとに空所の数が増え、難易度が増します。

☞音声を聞き、空所部分を書き取ってください。音声は何度聞いても構いません。

## ▶頻出単語チェック！：

・各Unitのトピックに頻出し、当該Unitでも使用されている語句をチェックします。

・リスニングとリーディングの両セクションの最初のページに8語ずつあります。

☞見出し語句と適切な意味（英語）を選びます。意味は本文で使われている意味が表示されています。

## ▶各Partの構成：

　全Partに"Check Point!"があります。何を学ぶのか、どのような能力を身に付ければよいのかを明示しました。

# LISTENING SECTION

- Part 1は、He, She, The man, The womanなどに加え人物以外の主語も取り上げています。
- Part 2は、質問文に頻出する疑問詞を中心とした構成になっています。
- Part 3は、会話の内容や目的、誰と誰の会話かなどの概略を問う質

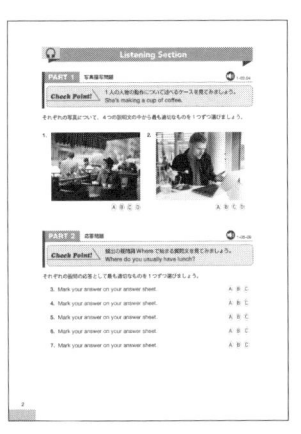

問文を例題の最初に取り上げています。男女2名の会話を聞いて回答する問題を中心に、図表を見ながら回答する問題、話し手の意図を問う問題も登場します。
- Part 4は、説明文の主旨や主題、目的などの概略を問う質問文を問題の最初に取り上げています。音声と印刷された図表の情報を関連づけて回答する質問や、話し手の意図を問う質問もUnit 6以降に採用しています。
- ☞ Warm up同様に音声は成美堂ホームページ (https://www.seibido.co.jp/ad646) よりダウンロードあるいはスマートフォンやタブレットでストリーミング再生してください。

## ▶Grammar Review：

- 文法項目を頻度順に復習します。
- ☞各項目の説明を読み、続く例題に取り組みましょう。

## READING SECTION

- Part 5は、5つの問題のうち、最初の3つが文法問題、残り2つが語彙問題です。文法問題は前ページのGrammar Reviewで学んだ内容が問われています。語彙問題は頻度の高い品詞を取り上げています。
- Part 6は、3つの空所のうち、2つは文法問題や語彙問題で、1つが文挿入問題です。

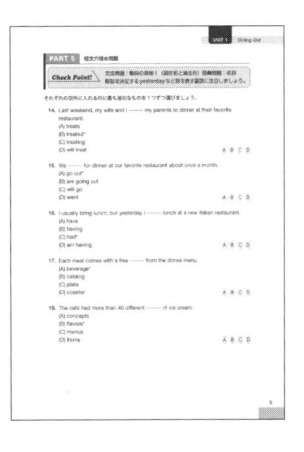

・Part 7は、出題頻度の高いEメールやメモ、手紙、広告文などを取り上げています。それぞれの説明文の主旨や主題、目的などの概略を問う質問文が問題の最初に出題されています。また、最近出題されるようになったテキストメッセージやオンラインチャット形式の問題や複数の文書を読んで解答する問題、さらに書き手の意図を問う質問や1文を挿入する文挿入問題を採用しています。

☞Part 5〜Part 7までは、目安の制限時間を設けて取り組みましょう。

Part 5 ---- 3分45秒（45秒@1問）

Part 6 ---- 2分30秒（50秒@1問）

Part 7 ---- 1分40秒（50秒@1問）←1つの文書

3分00秒（60秒@1問）←2つの文書

4分00秒（80秒@1問）←3つの文書

## ◎巻末『TOEIC必須複合名詞100』と『TOEIC重要熟語100』

巻末付録として『TOEIC必須複合名詞100』を付けました。知っている単語が2つ並ぶと知らない単語に変身してしまいます。リスニングやリーディングをスムーズに進めるためにもぜひ覚えてください。また『TOEIC重要熟語100』には例文も付けましたので音読しながら覚えましょう。

☑ボックスを付けておきましたので、知らないものがあったら必ず覚えましょう。

## ●TESTUDY **TESTUDY**

本書ではTESTUDY（=TEST+STUDY）という「e-learning+オンラインテスト」システムがご利用いただけます。

1. e-Learning：各Unitの復習ができます。（標準学習時間=30分）

2. Unit Review：各Unitのリスニングセクションをベースにしたディクテーション問題です。（標準学習時間=15分）

3. Extra Test：オンラインテストです。（標準学習時間=50分）

☞全て教員の指示に従って学習・受験してください。

# 目 次

**巻末付録：TOEIC必須複合名詞100**

**巻末付録：TOEIC重要熟語100**

# UNIT 1 Dining Out

## :: Warm up | Dictation Practice  1-02

それぞれの空所に入る語を、音声を聞いて書き入れてみましょう。

1. Do (                    ) sell soup?
2. She ordered (                    ) favorite dish.
3. Please let (                    ) decide.
4. Could you refill (                    ) glasses, please?
5. This is (                    ) seat.
6. Can (                    ) see the menu?
7. Could you bring (                    ) some water?
8. Everyone finished (                    ) drinks.

> ### 🔍 Points to Dictate
>
> 空所には1語が入ります。すべて代名詞です。ここでは1文を切り取って表示していますが、人称代名詞は会話や文の前後関係があって使われます。誰のことを指すのかが明白なので弱く速く、さらに前後の音のつながりで多様に変化します。

## ☑️ 頻出単語チェック！ Listening Section

単語と意味を品詞に気をつけながら結びつけてみましょう。

1. laptop (      )
2. pour (      )
3. vegetarian [adj.] (      )
4. client (      )
5. mark [v.] (      )
6. confirm (      )
7. location (      )
8. focus [v.] (      )

a. to give all your attention to something
b. a place
c. a person who receives services from a company
d. to move liquid from a container to another place (e.g., from a bottle into a cup)
e. a small computer that people can carry
f. to check if something is true
g. to show where something is with a drawing or symbol
h. not including meat

# Listening Section

## PART 1 　写真描写問題　 1-03,04

> **Check Point!** 　1人の人物の動作について述べるケースを見てみましょう。
> She's making a cup of coffee.

それぞれの写真について、4つの説明文の中から最も適切なものを1つずつ選びましょう。

**1.**

Ⓐ Ⓑ Ⓒ Ⓓ

**2.**

Ⓐ Ⓑ Ⓒ Ⓓ

## PART 2 　応答問題　 1-05-09

> **Check Point!** 　頻出の疑問詞 Where で始まる質問文を見てみましょう。
> Where do you usually have lunch?

それぞれの設問の応答として最も適切なものを1つずつ選びましょう。

**3.** Mark your answer on your answer sheet. 　Ⓐ Ⓑ Ⓒ

**4.** Mark your answer on your answer sheet. 　Ⓐ Ⓑ Ⓒ

**5.** Mark your answer on your answer sheet. 　Ⓐ Ⓑ Ⓒ

**6.** Mark your answer on your answer sheet. 　Ⓐ Ⓑ Ⓒ

**7.** Mark your answer on your answer sheet. 　Ⓐ Ⓑ Ⓒ

 **PART 3** 会話問題  1-10,11

> ***Check Point!***  男性が何について尋ねているのか大きく捉えましょう。
> What does the man ask about?

会話についての設問に対し、最も適切なものを1つずつ選びましょう。

**8.** What does the man ask about?
   (A) The opening time of the restaurant
   (B) The types of dishes on the menu
   (C) The prices of different dishes
   (D) The location of the restaurant

**9.** What does the woman offer to do?
   (A) Send the man a menu
   (B) Cook some special food
   (C) Reserve some dishes
   (D) Make a reservation

**10.** What will the man probably do next?
   (A) Come to the restaurant
   (B) Speak to his coworkers
   (C) Find another restaurant
   (D) Book a table for dinner

**PART 4** 説明文問題  1-12,13

> ***Check Point!***  この広告が何の広告なのか大きく捉えましょう。
> What is the advertisement mainly about?

説明文についての設問に対し、最も適切なものを1つずつ選びましょう。

**11.** What is the advertisement mainly about?
   (A) A restaurant
   (B) A cleaning company
   (C) A catering service
   (D) A conference hall

**12.** What does the speaker say about the food?
   (A) They can make whatever people need.
   (B) They only serve cold food.
   (C) They bring it to customers very quickly.
   (D) They cook very good dishes.

**13.** What does the speaker ask the listeners to do?
   (A) Contact the company
   (B) Work for the company
   (C) Come to an event
   (D) Try some food

## Grammar Review　動詞の時制 1：現在形、過去形

■**現在形**は変わらない事実や、繰り返される習慣を表します。この形は usually, always, often, sometimes, rarely, never, daily, weekly, every day など頻度を表す副詞と一緒に使われることが多いです。She *often* **eats** at that restaurant.（彼女はよくそのレストランで食事を<u>します</u>［習慣］）。

■**過去形**（動詞 +ed など）：は過去の特定の時点に起こった出来事を表します。yesterday, previously, before, then, (two days) ago など過去を表す副詞と一緒に使われることが多いです。We **had** pizza *yesterday*.（昨日、私たちはピザを食べ<u>ました</u>）。

《例題》各空所に入れるべき最も適切な語句を 1 つ選んで、その記号を答えなさい。

1. I usually ------- my guests to this restaurant to have lunch.
   (A) inviting　　(B) invited　　(C) will invite　　(D) invite

2. We ------- Beth with a birthday cake at the restaurant last Sunday.
   (A) surprise　　(B) surprises　　(C) surprised　　(D) surprising

## Reading Section

### ✔ 頻出単語チェック！　Reading Section

単語と意味を品詞に気をつけながら結びつけてみましょう。

1. treat [v.] (　　)
2. beverage (　　)
3. diner (　　)
4. traditional (　　)
5. recipe (　　)
6. tasty (　　)
7. healthy (　　)
8. run [v.] (　　)

a. things done in the same way for a long time
b. an instruction that tells you how to cook food
c. a cheap, casual restaurant
d. delicious
e. to pay for something for someone
f. to manage or operate a business
g. good for your body
h. a drink

**PART 5**　短文穴埋め問題

**Check Point!**　文法問題：動詞の時制1（現在形と過去形）、語彙問題：名詞
時制を決定するyesterdayなど時を表す副詞に注目しましょう。

それぞれの空所に入れるのに最も適切なものを1つずつ選びましょう。

**14.** Last weekend, my wife and I ------- my parents to dinner at their favorite
restaurant.
(A) treats
(B) treated
(C) treating
(D) will treat
Ⓐ Ⓑ Ⓒ Ⓓ

**15.** We ------- next to a great restaurant so we go there about once a month.
(A) live
(B) living
(C) will live
(D) lived
Ⓐ Ⓑ Ⓒ Ⓓ

**16.** I usually bring lunch, but yesterday I ------- lunch at a new Italian restaurant.
(A) have
(B) having
(C) had
(D) am having
Ⓐ Ⓑ Ⓒ Ⓓ

**17.** Each meal comes with a free ------- from the drinks menu.
(A) beverage
(B) catalog
(C) plate
(D) cup
Ⓐ Ⓑ Ⓒ Ⓓ

**18.** The café had more than 40 different ------- of ice cream.
(A) concepts
(B) flavors
(C) menus
(D) items
Ⓐ Ⓑ Ⓒ Ⓓ

**Check Point!**   メモ　語彙問題：接続詞、前置詞
文挿入問題：空所の前までの流れと矛盾のないものを選びましょう。

それぞれの空所に入れるのに最も適切なものを1つずつ選びましょう。

---

**To:** All Staff
**From:** Amanda Littlejohn
**Date:** May 1
**Subject:** Invitation to company dinner

---

Dear All,

As you know, this year is our company's fiftieth year, ------- **19.** I would like to invite you all to a company dinner.

The meal will be at the Riverside Hotel at 6:00 P.M. on Friday, June 12. The company will pay for your food and your first drink. ------- **20.**

If you are able to attend, please let us know by sending an e-mail to Helen Moore ------- **21.** May 14.

I hope to see you all there.

Best wishes,

Amanda Littlejohn
President
Speedway Motors

**19.** (A) but
(B) as
(C) so
(D) for

**20.** (A) After that, please pay for any other drinks by yourself.
(B) So, please send the money before the dinner.
(C) However, you must pay for all your own drinks.
(D) Second, you should wear nice clothes for the dinner.

**21.** (A) for
(B) by
(C) at
(D) in

> **Check Point!** 記事（1つの文書、2つの質問）
> 何を知らせる記事なのか、その要点を確認しましょう。

文章を読んで、それぞれの設問の答えとして最も適切なものを1つずつ選びましょう。

---

### Vietnamese Restaurant Now Open

A new Vietnamese restaurant, Saigon Diner, has just opened on Hanover Street. Owner Hong Thi Tran moved to Toronto from Vietnam last year.

"All of the dishes that we serve are traditional Vietnamese recipes," she said. "We use a lot of fresh meat and vegetables, so everything is very tasty and very healthy."

Tran worked as a chef in Saigon before marrying a Canadian who was working in Vietnam. He works for a large bank in the city. Tran says she is enjoying living in Canada, but the weather is colder than in Vietnam!

---

**22.** According to the article, what is true about Saigon Diner?
   (A) It opened in the city last year.
   (B) It is run by a husband and wife.
   (C) It serves traditional Vietnamese food.
   (D) It is owned by a Canadian man.

**23.** Where did Ms. Tran work in Vietnam?
   (A) At a bank
   (B) At a restaurant
   (C) At a supermarket
   (D) At a travel company

# UNIT 2 General Business

## **Warm up**   Dictation Practice    1-14

それぞれの空所に入る語を、音声を聞いて書き入れてみましょう。

1. (　　　　　　　　) you finish the report?
2. The manager is (　　　　　　) Japan.
3. I (　　　　　　) meet you at the office.
4. I have a meeting (　　　　　　) 10 A.M.
5. She (　　　　　　) go on the business trip.
6. Are there (　　　　　　) changes to the schedule?
7. When (　　　　　　) the meeting start?
8. Frank (　　　　　　) Janet work in the same department.

> 🔍 **Points to Dictate**
>
> ここでは助動詞、接続詞、前置詞などの「機能語」と呼ばれるものの聞き取りです。機能語は文の主要部分を構成する名詞や動詞などと異なり弱く短く、時にはほとんど聞こえないことがあります。どのように弱く短く発話されるのか慣れることが大切です。

☑️ 頻出単語チェック！  **Listening Section**

語句と意味を品詞に気をつけながら結びつけてみましょう。

1. lean against (　　)
2. conference (　　)
3. contract [n.] (　　)
4. agency (　　)
5. worried [adj.] (　　)
6. go over (　　)
7. feedback [n.] (　　)
8. hire [v.] (　　)

a. to rest on something for support
b. feeling bad because you think that something bad will happen
c. an event where many people give presentations
d. to look at something carefully
e. a document that people sign to make an agreement about something
f. to give someone a job
g. comments about the good and/or bad points of something
h. a company that provides a service to other companies

# Listening Section

## PART 1 　写真描写問題

 1-15,16

**Check Point!**　1人の人物の動作について述べるケースを見てみましょう。
A man is leaning against the desk.

それぞれの写真について、4つの説明文の中から最も適切なものを1つずつ選びましょう。

1.

Ⓐ Ⓑ Ⓒ Ⓓ

2.

Ⓐ Ⓑ Ⓒ Ⓓ

## PART 2 　応答問題

1-17-21

**Check Point!**　頻出の疑問詞 Who で始まる質問文を見てみましょう。
Who's attending the meeting on Thursday?

それぞれの設問の応答として最も適切なものを1つずつ選びましょう。

3. Mark your answer on your answer sheet.　Ⓐ Ⓑ Ⓒ

4. Mark your answer on your answer sheet.　Ⓐ Ⓑ Ⓒ

5. Mark your answer on your answer sheet.　Ⓐ Ⓑ Ⓒ

6. Mark your answer on your answer sheet.　Ⓐ Ⓑ Ⓒ

7. Mark your answer on your answer sheet.　Ⓐ Ⓑ Ⓒ

## PART 3 会話問題

 1-22,23

***Check Point!*** 2人の話し手が何について話し合っているのか大きく捉えましょう。
What are the speakers mainly discussing?

会話についての設問に対し、最も適切なものを1つずつ選びましょう。

8. What are the speakers mainly discussing?
   (A) Arranging a meeting
   (B) Preparing for a presentation
   (C) Receiving customer feedback
   (D) Buying some products

9. What does the woman suggest?
   (A) Practicing together
   (B) Listening to the sales people
   (C) Reserving a meeting room
   (D) Meeting with their boss

10. What will the speakers do tomorrow?
    (A) Have an important sales meeting
    (B) Reserve a meeting room for next week
    (C) Prepare for the meeting
    (D) Discuss how the meeting went

## PART 4 説明文問題

 1-24,25

***Check Point!*** 話し手がどこで働いているのか聞き取りましょう。
Where does the speaker most likely work?

説明文についての設問に対し、最も適切なものを1つずつ選びましょう。

11. Where does the speaker most likely work?
    (A) At a travel company
    (B) At a clothes company
    (C) At a supermarket chain
    (D) At a construction company

12. Who most likely are the listeners?
    (A) Customers
    (B) Company employees
    (C) Store managers
    (D) Visitors to the office

13. What will the listeners most likely do next?
    (A) Talk about the factory
    (B) Discuss sales in France
    (C) Meet the sales teams
    (D) Plan a special event

■ **現在進行形**（be 動詞 + 動詞 -ing 形）：は、まさに進行中の動作や一時的な行動を表します。now, today, at the moment, right now など今を表す副詞（句）と一緒に使われます。

The team **is working** on a new project *at the moment*.（現在チームは新しいプロジェクトに<u>取り組んでいる</u>）。

■ **現在完了形**（have+ 過去分詞）：は過去の出来事が現在に影響を与えていることを示します。already, before, just, yet などの副詞や、since「〜以来」、for「〜の間」などの前置詞句と一緒に使われ、完了・経験・継続を表します。

The manager **has arranged** the meeting with the clients *already*.（マネージャーは既にクライアントとの会議を<u>設定しました</u>［完了]）。

《例題》各空所に入れるべき最も適切な語句を 1 つ選んで、その記号を答えなさい。

**1.** Our team ------- a presentation for the client today.
   (A) prepares    (B) prepared    (C) is preparing    (D) preparing

**2.** The company ------- the new advertising campaign yet.
   (A) doesn't start    (B) wasn't starting    (C) hasn't been starting
   (D) hasn't started

# Reading Section

## ✓ 頻出単語チェック！ **Reading Section**

単語と意味を品詞に気をつけながら結びつけてみましょう。

**1.** several (   )        **a.** in another country
**2.** overseas (   )      **b.** some, but not a lot of
**3.** respect [v.] (   )    **c.** to buy something
**4.** expand (   )       **d.** to give someone an idea about what to do
**5.** share [v.] (   )     **e.** to make something bigger
**6.** purchase [v.] (   )   **f.** to give something to other people
**7.** suggest (   )       **g.** to think someone is good or has good ideas
**8.** specific (   )      **h.** particular; not any

## PART 5    短文穴埋め問題

**Check Point!**    文法問題：動詞の時制2（現在進行形と現在完了形）、語彙問題：動詞
時制を決定する now など時を表す副詞に注目しましょう。

それぞれの空所に入れるのに最も適切なものを1つずつ選びましょう。

**14.** She ------- in the marketing department since last September.
(A) has worked
(B) is working
(C) will work
(D) worked

ⒶⒷⒸⒹ

**15.** At the moment, I ------- for jobs with several large engineering companies.
(A) apply
(B) am applying
(C) applied
(D) will apply

ⒶⒷⒸⒹ

**16.** My sister ------- overseas for more than ten years.
(A) works
(B) is working
(C) has worked
(D) is worked

ⒶⒷⒸⒹ

**17.** I really ------- her because she is always very well prepared for our meetings.
(A) project
(B) respect
(C) protect
(D) inspect

ⒶⒷⒸⒹ

**18.** The company aims to ------- by opening some more branches.
(A) expand
(B) stay
(C) reduce
(D) forget

ⒶⒷⒸⒹ

それぞれの空所に入れるのに最も適切なものを 1 つずつ選びましょう。

---

**To:** All Team Members
**From:** Jeremy Brown
**Date:** February 17
**Subject:** Plan for March Team Meeting

---

Dear All,

We will have our next team meeting on March 7, ------- **19.** I am writing to share the plan for the meeting with you.

We have two points to discuss:

1. Reports about everyone's projects
2. Information about new projects

------- **20.** If yes, please let me know by e-mail.

I'll ------- **21.** you about the time and location of the meeting next week.

Many thanks,

Jeremy

---

**19.** (A) but
(B) so
(C) because
(D) or

**20.** (A) What other topics would you like to discuss?
(B) I'm looking forward to discussing these together.
(C) Please tell me about other discussion topics.
(D) Does anyone want to add a discussion topic?

**21.** (A) find
(B) inform
(C) teach
(D) give

文章を読んで、それぞれの設問の答えとして最も適切なものを1つずつ選びましょう。

---

### 10% Off Your Hotel Room!

Thank you for purchasing your tickets for this year's Business Technology Conference. Because you bought your tickets early, we are giving you 10% off your hotel room in Las Vegas.

To get this discount, when you reserve your hotel, use the code: BTCVEGAS10

We strongly suggest that you reserve your hotel as soon as possible, because there will be two other conferences in Las Vegas on the same weekend.

The Business Technology Conference will be held at the Las Vegas Conference Center. See www.las-vegas-conference-center.com/map for a map of the area.

---

**22.** What is the purpose of the notice?
(A) To give details about a special offer
(B) To invite people to a special event
(C) To promote a new travel package
(D) To announce a change in the conference schedule

**23.** What does the notice indicate about the discount?
(A) Customers must book right away.
(B) A special code must be used.
(C) It is for one company only.
(D) Visiting a Web site is necessary.

# UNIT 3 Manufacturing

## ⋮⋮ *Warm up* — Dictation Practice — 1-26

それぞれの空所に入る語（ここでは全て短縮形）を、音声を聞いて書き入れてみましょう。

1. (          ) making parts for the new machine.
2. (          ) the next step in the process?
3. They (       ) finish the order by Friday.
4. (          ) checking the quality of the materials.
5. (          ) worked on similar products in the past.
6. (          ) completed the order for 500 units.
7. (          ) responsible for the schedule?
8. (          ) the manual for this machine?

### 🔍 Points to Dictate

助動詞や疑問詞、be 動詞などを含む短縮形の聞き取りです。She has と She is の短縮形＝ She's のように形が同じものがあります。また、can't のように can と 180 度意味が異なる短縮形にも要注意です。自分でも言えるように練習しましょう。

## ✔️ 頻出単語チェック！ Listening Section

語句と意味を品詞に気をつけながら結びつけてみましょう。

1. stack [v.] (   )
2. factory (   )
3. side by side (   )
4. take a day off (   )
5. put away (   )
6. make sure (   )
7. supervisor (   )
8. pack [v.] (   )

a. a building where products are made
b. to not go to work and take a holiday
c. to put things into a bag or a box
d. to put something in a place because you do not need it now
e. a person who manages other people and checks their work
f. to put things one on top of another
g. to carefully check that you did something
h. next to each other

## PART 1　写真描写問題　 1-27,28

*Check Point!*　2人以上の人物の動作等について述べるケースを見てみましょう。
They're standing next to each other.

それぞれの写真について、4つの説明文の中から最も適切なものを1つずつ選びましょう。

1.

Ⓐ Ⓑ Ⓒ Ⓓ

2.

Ⓐ Ⓑ Ⓒ Ⓓ

## PART 2　応答問題　 1-29-33

*Check Point!*　頻出の疑問詞 When で始まる質問文を見てみましょう。
When's the next factory meeting?

それぞれの設問の応答として最も適切なものを1つずつ選びましょう。

**3.** Mark your answer on your answer sheet.　　Ⓐ Ⓑ Ⓒ

**4.** Mark your answer on your answer sheet.　　Ⓐ Ⓑ Ⓒ

**5.** Mark your answer on your answer sheet.　　Ⓐ Ⓑ Ⓒ

**6.** Mark your answer on your answer sheet.　　Ⓐ Ⓑ Ⓒ

**7.** Mark your answer on your answer sheet.　　Ⓐ Ⓑ Ⓒ

**PART 3** 会話問題  1-34,35

> **Check Point!** 男女の話し手のうちの1人が誰かを尋ねています。
> Who is the man?

会話についての設問に対し、最も適切なものを1つずつ選びましょう。

**8.** Who is the man?
(A) A hospital worker
(B) A delivery person
(C) The woman's coworker
(D) The woman's neighbor

**9.** What does the man say about Thursday?
(A) He can work all day.
(B) He cannot work in the afternoon.
(C) He needs the woman's help.
(D) He has to see the doctor.

**10.** What does the woman ask the man to do?
(A) Make a delivery
(B) Pack some boxes
(C) Book some appointments
(D) Work on Thursday afternoon

**PART 4** 説明文問題  1-36,37

> **Check Point!** 聞き手は誰か、その役割や状況に注目しましょう。
> Who most likely are the listeners?

説明文についての設問に対し、最も適切なものを1つずつ選びましょう。

**11.** Who most likely are the listeners?
(A) Customers
(B) Delivery drivers
(C) Factory workers
(D) Supervisors

**12.** What does the speaker ask the listeners to do?
(A) Look at the items
(B) Pack some boxes
(C) Store the items
(D) Write a report

**13.** According to the speaker, what is important about their products?
(A) Low prices
(B) Good quality
(C) Quick service
(D) Unusual items

■**過去進行形**（was+ 動詞 -ing 形）：は過去の特定の時点で進行中だった動作や出来事を表します。特定の時点（at 8 o'clock, at that time, when he arrived, など）を示す副詞句や副詞節を伴い、その時点で「〜していた」という意味を表します。The engineers **were testing** the machines *when the manager arrived*.（マネージャーが到着したとき、エンジニアたちは機械を<u>テストしていた</u>）。

■**過去完了形**（had+ 過去分詞）：は過去の一時点よりも前に起こった出来事の完了・経験・継続を表します。already, before などの副詞や since... 「〜以来」、for... 「〜の間」などの副詞句、when や before に導かれる副詞節を伴い、時間的な背景を示します。The staff **had** *already* **cleaned** the work area *when we arrived*.（我々が到着した時にはスタッフが既に作業エリアを<u>清掃し終わっていた</u>）。

《例題》各空所に入れるべき最も適切な語句を1つ選んで、その記号を答えなさい。

**1.** The workers ------- the new software when they found a big problem.
(A) test　　(B) tested　　(C) are testing　　(D) were testing

**2.** Before I visited the factory, the team ------- more than 1,000 products.
(A) had manufactured　　(B) manufactures　　(C) manufacturing
(D) manufacture

## Reading Section

### ✔ 頻出単語チェック！　Reading Section

語句と意味を品詞に気をつけながら結びつけてみましょう。

**1.** produce [v.] (　　)  　　**a.** agreement that you can do something
**2.** protect (　　)  　　**b.** to stop someone from getting hurt
**3.** replace (　　)  　　**c.** to change something for a similar thing
**4.** provide (　　)  　　**d.** to watch or listen carefully
**5.** employ [v.] (　　)  　　**e.** the things around you
**6.** permission (　　)  　　**f.** to give people jobs at a company
**7.** pay attention to (　　)  　　**g.** to make something
**8.** surroundings (　　)  　　**h.** to give something to someone

## PART 5    短文穴埋め問題

**Check Point!**

文法問題：動詞の時制 3（過去進行形、過去完了形）
語彙問題：動詞
was+ 動詞 -ing や had+ 過去分詞の形を見極めましょう。

それぞれの空所に入れるのに最も適切なものを1つずつ選びましょう。

**14.** They ------- their lunch when the new parts arrived.
   (A) eat
   (B) eaten
   (C) were eating
   (D) are eating                                Ⓐ Ⓑ Ⓒ Ⓓ

**15.** The team ------- over 20% of the order when we visited last Friday.
   (A) produce
   (B) is producing
   (C) has produced
   (D) had produced                              Ⓐ Ⓑ Ⓒ Ⓓ

**16.** When she got to the factory, most of the workers ------- yet.
   (A) don't arrive
   (B) didn't arrive
   (C) hasn't arrived
   (D) hadn't arrived                            Ⓐ Ⓑ Ⓒ Ⓓ

**17.** This clothing will ------- you when you are inside the factory.
   (A) protect
   (B) keep
   (C) wear
   (D) hold                                      Ⓐ Ⓑ Ⓒ Ⓓ

**18.** That machine cannot be fixed, so we need to ------- it.
   (A) replace
   (B) repair
   (C) restore
   (D) revise                                    Ⓐ Ⓑ Ⓒ Ⓓ

それぞれの空所に入れるのに最も適切なものを１つずつ選びましょう。

---

**PRESS RELEASE: New Bottle Factory to Open**

GREENFIELD (June 15) – Bottle maker Greenfield will open a new factory in Oaktown next year. The new factory will be two times larger ------- the current one. -------
**19.**　　　　　　　　　　　　　　　　　　　**20.**

Greenfield President Michael Walter said, "I was born in Oaktown, so it's important for me to be able to provide jobs for the people in this area. Greenfield ------- people in Oaktown for more than 30 years, and now we can
**21.**
hire more people as the company continues to grow."

---

**19.** (A) by
　　(B) as
　　(C) to
　　(D) than

**20.** (A) More than 100 new jobs will be created for local people.
　　(B) The company did not say when the new factory will open.
　　(C) This is very bad news for workers in the local area.
　　(D) The new factory will be smaller, but work will be faster.

**21.** (A) is employing
　　(B) is being employed
　　(C) has employed
　　(D) had been employed

## PART 7   読解問題

> **Check Point!**
>
> 掲示（1つの文書）、2つの質問
> 誰が何のために出した掲示なのか、その目的は何でしょう。

文章を読んで、それぞれの設問の答えとして最も適切なものを1つずつ選びましょう。

### Attention: Factory Visitors

For your safety, always wear safety boots, gloves, and yellow jackets inside the factory. Visitors can borrow these from the manager.

Do not touch any of the machines in this area, and do not try to move anything unless you have permission. If you want to use something, ask the factory manager first. There may be important safety rules to follow.

Please do not use your phone in the factory. It's important to pay attention to your surroundings so you can stay safe in this area.

**22.** What is the purpose of the sign?
   (A) To tell visitors how to use the machines
   (B) To inform visitors of the safety rules
   (C) To tell visitors about training courses
   (D) To request visitors use equipment

**23.** What is indicated about the safety items?
   (A) Visitors should ask the manager for them.
   (B) Visitors should buy their own.
   (C) Visitors need training to use them.
   (D) Visitors shouldn't use them.

# Finance and Budgeting

## Dictation Practice

 1-38

それぞれの空所に入る語を、音声を聞いて書き入れてみましょう。

1. We (              )(                        ) answer by noon.
2. He (              )(                    ) name to the list.
3. She (              )(                    ) notes to the file.
4. I (              )(                  ) to sign this form.
5. The total cost (                )(                    ) plan is high.
6. He looked at the details (                )(                ) contract.
7. She asked (                )(              ) help.
8. The (                )(                    ) the project increased.

---

### 🔍 Points to Dictate

２つの語が連続して１語のように聞こえるケースの練習です。ここでは動
詞＋代名詞、前置詞＋代名詞、名詞＋前置詞を聞き取りましょう。ここで
最も大切なのは、動詞の時制や代名詞の his/her, you/your などを前後関
係を考え正確に聞き取れるようになることです。

---

☑ **頻出単語チェック！** **Listening Section**

語句と意味を品詞に気をつけながら結びつけてみましょう。

1. check out [v.] (      )
2. section [n.] (      )
3. quit (      )
4. order [n.] (      )
5. approve (      )
6. budget [n.] (      )
7. space [n.] (      )
8. facility (      )

a. leave a job
b. to look at
c. a building used for a special purpose
d. a request to a company to buy their products or services
e. an area that is empty and available to be used for something
f. a part of a company
g. the money provided to do something
h. to say that something can happen

# Listening Section

## PART 1  写真描写問題

 1-39,40

> *Check Point!* 複数の人物のうちの1人または複数の動作を見てみましょう。
> They're looking at each other.

それぞれの写真について、4つの説明文の中から最も適切なものを1つずつ選びましょう。

**1.**

Ⓐ Ⓑ Ⓒ Ⓓ

**2.**

Ⓐ Ⓑ Ⓒ Ⓓ

## PART 2  応答問題

 1-41-45

> *Check Point!* 頻出の疑問詞 Why で始まる質問文を見てみましょう。
> Why are you attending the workshop?

それぞれの設問の応答として最も適切なものを1つずつ選びましょう。

**3.** Mark your answer on your answer sheet.　　Ⓐ Ⓑ Ⓒ

**4.** Mark your answer on your answer sheet.　　Ⓐ Ⓑ Ⓒ

**5.** Mark your answer on your answer sheet.　　Ⓐ Ⓑ Ⓒ

**6.** Mark your answer on your answer sheet.　　Ⓐ Ⓑ Ⓒ

**7.** Mark your answer on your answer sheet.　　Ⓐ Ⓑ Ⓒ

> **Check Point!**　2人の会話で問題となっていることを聞き取りましょう。
> What is the problem?

会話についての設問に対し、最も適切なものを1つずつ選びましょう。

**8.** What is the problem?
(A) The meeting was delayed.
(B) The project was not approved.
(C) The meeting was canceled.
(D) The budget was not increased.

**9.** Who most likely is the woman?
(A) A project manager
(B) A bank clerk
(C) A salesperson
(D) A supplier

**10.** What does the man suggest doing?
(A) Offering a discount
(B) Promising a big order
(C) Asking for a discount
(D) Finding another supplier

> **Check Point!**　何についてのアナウンスか大きく捉えましょう。
> What is the announcement about?

説明文についての設問に対し、最も適切なものを1つずつ選びましょう。

**11.** What is the announcement about?
(A) A new parking area
(B) A new train line
(C) A new bus station
(D) A new park

**12.** What problem does the speaker mention?
(A) Not enough money
(B) Too little space
(C) No available staff
(D) Needing more time

**13.** When is the facility scheduled to open?
(A) May
(B) July
(C) August
(D) October

## ✍ Grammar Review 名詞とその派生語

■**名詞**は主語や目的語、補語として文章の中で最も重要な役割を担います。名詞を効率的に覚えるにはリーディングを通じて文章の前後関係の中で学ぶことが効果的です。

▶さらに**派生語**を覚えることで、その数が数倍に膨れ上がります。例えば名詞の use（使用）を考えると語幹（use）に続く接尾辞を変えることで、us*er*（使用者）、us*age*（使用法）、use*fulness*（有用性）、us*ability*（使いやすさ）のように 4 つの別の名詞になります。また、接頭辞を付けることでも *mis*use（誤用）、*re*use（再利用）のように異なる名詞が生まれます。さらに異なる接尾辞や接頭辞を付けることで異なる品詞にもなりますので、その形を覚えると圧倒的な語彙力が身に付きます。以下に、名詞を作る接尾辞と接頭辞をまとめます。

▶名詞を作る接尾辞：-ness, -er/-or, -tion/-sion, -ment, -ist, -ship, -ty/-ity, -ant, -ence/-ance, -ry, -age など

名詞を作る接頭辞：bi-, un-, re-, pre-, post-, mis-, co-, inter-, in-, ex- など

---

《例題》次の空所に入れるべき最も適切な語を 1 つ選んで、その記号を答えなさい。

**1.** The new manager is known for her -------.
(A) lead　　(B) leader　　(C) leadership　　(D) leading

**2.** The ------- was filled with interesting ideas.
(A) discuss　　(B) discussion　　(C) discussing　　(D) discussed

---

# Reading Section

### ☑ 頻出単語チェック！ Reading Section

語句と意味を品詞に気をつけながら結びつけてみましょう。

1. investment (　　)
2. reduce (　　)
3. expense (　　)
4. total amount (　　)
5. corrected (　　)
6. right away (　　)
7. branch [n.] (　　)
8. CEO (　　)

**a.** money spent by a person for their work (e.g., for travel)

**b.** an office or shop that is part of a group owned by the same company

**c.** now; immediately

**d.** to make something smaller in size or number

**e.** money that is used to try to make more money

**f.** the result after all the numbers in a list are added together

**g.** the leader of a company (Chief Executive Officer)

**h.** changed so that it is not wrong

**PART 5** 短文穴埋め問題

> **Check Point!**
> 文法問題：名詞とその派生語　語彙問題：動詞
> 名詞を作る接尾辞、接頭辞を覚えておきましょう。

それぞれの空所に入れるのに最も適切なものを1つずつ選びましょう。

**14.** Thank you again for your ------- with this month's financial report.
(A) assisting
(B) assistant
(C) assisted
(D) assistance　　　　　　　　　　　　　　　Ⓐ Ⓑ Ⓒ Ⓓ

**15.** After the ------- of the sales report, we will have a meeting to discuss it.
(A) complete
(B) completion
(C) completed
(D) completing　　　　　　　　　　　　　　Ⓐ Ⓑ Ⓒ Ⓓ

**16.** The CEO is hoping to receive some ------- from a larger company.
(A) invest
(B) investor
(C) investing
(D) investment　　　　　　　　　　　　　　Ⓐ Ⓑ Ⓒ Ⓓ

**17.** The company plans to ------- its costs to increase profits.
(A) reduce
(B) build
(C) ignore
(D) sell　　　　　　　　　　　　　　　　　　Ⓐ Ⓑ Ⓒ Ⓓ

**18.** It seems that the company's sales ------- by over $2 million last year.
(A) dropped
(B) failed
(C) lost
(D) missed　　　　　　　　　　　　　　　　Ⓐ Ⓑ Ⓒ Ⓓ

28

## PART 6  長文穴埋め問題

**Check Point!** Eメール　語彙問題：接続詞、動詞
文挿入問題：直前の文章では問題点が指摘されています。

それぞれの空所に入れるのに最も適切なものを１つずつ選びましょう。

---

**To:** Norman Shaw <n.shaw@flower-imports.com>
**From:** Marianne Blanc <m.blanc@flower-imports.com>
**Date:** August 23
**Subject:** Re: Business Trip Expense Form (New York Trip)

---

Hi Norman,

Thank you for sending me your business trip expense form.

-------, I am writing to tell you that I found an error. The total amount on the
**19.**
form does not match the total of your receipts. -------- If you did, you need to
**20.**
change the total amount on the form.

Please ------- this error and send the corrected form right away.
**21.**

Best regards,

Marianne Blanc

---

**19.** (A) However
(B) Sometimes
(C) First
(D) Therefore

**20.** (A) You do not need to make any
changes here.
(B) How did you pay for
everything?
(C) Please check that you sent me
all of the receipts.
(D) However, I have not received
these from you yet.

**21.** (A) ignore
(B) fix
(C) break
(D) cover

**Check Point!** テキストメッセージ（1つの文書、2つの質問）
Amelia が何のために連絡を取ったかに注目しましょう。

文章を読んで、それぞれの設問の答えとして最も適切なものを1つずつ選びましょう。

| Amelia | 9:17 A.M. |
|---|---|
| Are you in the office? | |

| Ryan | 9:18 A.M. |
|---|---|
| I'll be there in about thirty minutes. Why? | |

| Amelia | 9:19 A.M. |
|---|---|
| I'm going to be about 15 minutes late, because I need to go to the bank. | |

| Ryan | 9:20 A.M. |
|---|---|
| OK. That's no problem. | |

| Amelia | 9:20 A.M. |
|---|---|
| Thanks. You know what? The branch I usually go to is closed today so I have to go to another one on the other side of town. | |

| Ryan | 9:21 A.M. |
|---|---|
| That's too bad. | |

| Amelia | 9:21 A.M. |
|---|---|
| Yeah. Well, I need to take care of this today, so I'll try to be quick. | |

| Ryan | 9:22 A.M. |
|---|---|
| OK. That's fine. I'll tell the rest of the team that you will be a little late. | |

| Amelia | 9:22 A.M. |
|---|---|
| Thank you. I'll be there as soon as I can. | |

**22.** Why did Amelia contact her coworker?

  (A) To complain about a problem

  (B) To check the meeting schedule

  (C) To arrange a meeting

  (D) To tell him she will be late

**23.** At 9:20 A.M., what does Amelia mean when she writes "You know what"?

  (A) She is suggesting a new idea.

  (B) She thinks Ryan knows something.

  (C) She's telling Ryan she has surprising news.

  (D) She needs some information.

# UNIT 5 Communication

それぞれの空所に入る語を、音声を聞いて書き入れてみましょう。短縮形は1語とします。

1. I (      ) (      ) now.
2. (      ) (      ) listening.
3. (      ) (      ) later.
4. We (      ) (      ) it soon.
5. I'll (      ) (      ) know.
6. She (      ) (      ) soon.
7. Is (      ) (      ) OK for you?
8. We're happy (      ) (      ) results.

### Points to Dictate

前の単語の最後の音と、次の単語の最初の音が同じ場合に、一方の音が脱落してしまうケースを練習しましょう。例えば、stop paying(p+p) は≒ stopaying のように、hot topic(t+t) は≒ hotopic のように聞こえます。

### ✔ 頻出単語チェック！ Listening Section

語句と意味を品詞に気をつけながら結びつけてみましょう。

1. fill out (   )     a. to like something better than something
2. package [n.] (   )     b. small card with your name and contact
3. business card (   )     information
4. plenty (   )     c. a box with items inside, often sent by mail
5. prefer (   )     d. a big room for large meetings
6. conference room (   )     e. to write all the information in a form
7. prepare (   )     f. to give someone some work to do
8. assign (   )     g. a lot of something
            h. to get ready for something

**Listening Section**

PART 1    写真描写問題
 1-51,52

**Check Point!** 男性女性、複数いる中の1人の動作を見てみましょう。
One of the women is talking on the phone.

それぞれの写真について、4つの説明文の中から最も適切なものを1つずつ選びましょう。

**1.**   Ⓐ Ⓑ Ⓒ Ⓓ

**2.**   Ⓐ Ⓑ Ⓒ Ⓓ

PART 2    応答問題
 1-53-57

**Check Point!** 頻出の疑問詞 Which で始まる質問文を見てみましょう。
Which meeting room is available?

それぞれの設問の応答として最も適切なものを1つずつ選びましょう。

**3.** Mark your answer on your answer sheet.    Ⓐ Ⓑ Ⓒ

**4.** Mark your answer on your answer sheet.    Ⓐ Ⓑ Ⓒ

**5.** Mark your answer on your answer sheet.    Ⓐ Ⓑ Ⓒ

**6.** Mark your answer on your answer sheet.    Ⓐ Ⓑ Ⓒ

**7.** Mark your answer on your answer sheet.    Ⓐ Ⓑ Ⓒ

> **Check Point!** 話し手の一方が何について説明しているのか大きく捉えましょう。
> What does the woman explain to the man?

会話についての設問に対し、最も適切なものを1つずつ選びましょう。

**8.** What does the woman explain to the man?
- (A) The schedule for the project
- (B) The time and place of a meeting
- (C) The tasks they have been assigned
- (D) The problem that she is having

**9.** What will the man most likely do next?
- (A) Reserve a meeting room
- (B) Print some documents
- (C) Prepare for the meeting
- (D) Talk with Ken

**10.** Why does the woman say, "No problem"?
- (A) To show she is happy to help
- (B) To tell the man she is not angry
- (C) To show she has completed a task
- (D) To accept the man's thanks

> **Check Point!** メッセージの目的は何か大きく捉えましょう。
> What is the purpose of the message?

説明文についての設問に対し、最も適切なものを1つずつ選びましょう。

**11.** What is the purpose of the message?
- (A) To hire someone
- (B) To change something
- (C) To correct something
- (D) To check something

**12.** What does the man say about hiring staff?
- (A) They cannot hire anyone
- (B) They hired someone.
- (C) He doesn't know if it's OK.
- (D) He thinks no new staff are needed.

**13.** What will the listener most likely do next?
- (A) Contact the speaker
- (B) Ask someone else
- (C) Hire someone
- (D) Send a message to Mike

## ✎ Grammar Review 代名詞（人称代名詞・所有代名詞・再帰代名詞）

■**人称代名詞**は人・物を示します。一人称なら主格 (I)・所有格 (my)・目的格 (me) とあり、文中の働きによって、どの格になるかが決まります。**I** left **my** bag at home, so please wait for **me** here.（<u>私は</u>、<u>私の</u>バッグを家に忘れてきたので、ここで<u>私を</u>待っていてください）

■**所有代名詞**は「～のもの」を１語で表します。This is not **mine**.（これは<u>私のもの</u>ではありません）

■**再帰代名詞**は「～自身」を表す代名詞で、-self（複数形は -selves）が付きます。

Please introduce **yourself** to the new employees.（新入社員に<u>自己紹介</u>をしてください）

このように動詞の目的語として用いられる他、名詞や代名詞を強調することがあります。

*Susan* **herself** fixed the computer problem.（Susan は<u>自分で</u>コンピューターの問題を修理しました）。herself は Susan と同格に置かれて Susan を強調しています。

《例題》各空所に入れるべき最も適切な語を１つ選んで、その記号を答えなさい。

1. All team members must bring ------- laptops to the meeting.
   (A) they      (B) their      (C) them      (D) themselves

2. Jennifer wants to work on the report by ------- before showing it to her manager.
   (A) her      (B) herself      (C) hers      (D) she

## Reading Section

### ✔ 頻出単語チェック！ Reading Section

単語と意味を品詞に気をつけながら結びつけてみましょう。

1. submit (      )
2. respond (      )
3. operator (      )
4. retire (      )
5. stationery (      )
6. organization (      )
7. proud (      )
8. participate (      )

a. a group that works together to do something
b. to stop working forever
c. pens, pencils, rulers, erasers, etc.
d. a person that connects people using a phone system
e. pleased that you did something good
f. to do an activity with others
g. to give an important document to someone
h. to answer or reply

それぞれの空所に入れるのに最も適切なものを1つずつ選びましょう。

**14.** The manager asked us all to submit ------- reports to him by Friday.
(A) our
(B) us
(C) we
(D) ours
Ⓐ Ⓑ Ⓒ Ⓓ

**15.** Shall I send an e-mail to Greg or do you want to do it -------?
(A) himself
(B) myself
(C) ourselves
(D) yourself
Ⓐ Ⓑ Ⓒ Ⓓ

**16.** There's a cell phone on my desk, but it isn't -------.
(A) I
(B) me
(C) mine
(D) my
Ⓐ Ⓑ Ⓒ Ⓓ

**17.** It's important to ------- to a customer's e-mail within 24 hours.
(A) answer
(B) send
(C) proceed
(D) respond
Ⓐ Ⓑ Ⓒ Ⓓ

**18.** He called the company and asked the operator to ------- him to the IT department.
(A) change
(B) contact
(C) exchange
(D) transfer
Ⓐ Ⓑ Ⓒ Ⓓ

## PART 6   長文穴埋め問題

**Check Point!**    告知　語彙問題：接続詞　文法問題：動詞の語形
文挿入問題：各選択肢の頭にある接続詞に注目しましょう。

それぞれの空所に入れるのに最も適切なものを１つずつ選びましょう。

---

### CEO Travis Connor to Retire

CEO Travis Connor said that he will retire from the company at the end of this year. Travis has been our CEO for more than ten years, so we will miss him a lot when he leaves. ------- **19.**

I am sure Travis will want to thank you for your support over the years. So, ------- **20.** Travis leaves, we will have a party for him. Details of this event will ------- **21.** with you next week.

The company will announce the new CEO very soon.

---

**19.** (A) So, he thinks it's time for him to retire.
　　(B) Also, we are very sad that he is leaving.
　　(C) However, we hope he has a good retirement.
　　(D) Actually, he will stay with us for ten more years.

**20.** (A) before
　　(B) during
　　(C) while
　　(D) unless

**21.** (A) share
　　(B) sharing
　　(C) shared
　　(D) be shared

**Check Point!** 記事（1つの文書、2つの質問）
プロジェクトを誰が何のために始めたのか注目しましょう。

文章を読んで、それぞれの設問の答えとして最も適切なものを1つずつ選びましょう。

## Stationery Company to Help Children Around the World

Walker's Stationery said today that they will give thousands of products to help children from developing countries. Walker's is working with an organization called Education for Everyone. They will send pens, notebooks and other stationery products to schools in developing countries.

Walker's Stationery CEO Karl Donne decided to join the project right away when Education for Everyone asked him to participate. He said he is very proud that the company can help children around the world.

Walker's makes many kinds of stationery products. Their products are used in schools and offices across the United States.

**22.** According to the article, who came up with the idea to help children in developing countries?
(A) Walker's Stationery
(B) Schools around the world
(C) Education for Everyone
(D) Karl Donne

**23.** What is NOT true about Walker's Stationery?
(A) They make products for children and adults.
(B) They will give money to help schools in developing countries.
(C) They make notebooks as well as pens and pencils.
(D) They sell their products in the United States.

# UNIT 6

# Health

## Warm up　Dictation Practice　1-62

それぞれの空所に入る語を、音声を聞いて書き入れてみましょう。

1. She's trying to (　　　　　　) (　　　　　　) habits.
2. (　　　　　　) (　　　　　　) your teeth after every meal.
3. We'll (　　　　　) (　　　　　　) at a healthy restaurant.
4. It's important to (　　　　　) (　　　　　) exercise.
5. (　　　　　) (　　　　　) are on sale, please buy some.
6. This curry is (　　　　　) (　　　　　) and half meat.
7. He's going to (　　　　　) (　　　　　) care of his health.
8. I usually (　　　　　　) (　　　　　　) tea after breakfast.

## Points to Dictate

前の単語の最後の音と、次の単語の最初の音が同じ種類の場合に、一方の音が脱落してしまうケースを練習しましょう。p+b, t+d, f+v, k+g などで後ろの単語の最初の音が残ります。例えば、gap between (p+b) は≒ gabetween のように聞こえます。

## ✔ 頻出単語チェック！　Listening Section

単語と意味を品詞に気をつけながら結びつけてみましょう。

1. medicine (　　)
2. pick up (　　)
3. exactly (　　)
4. urgent (　　)
5. reschedule (　　)
6. receptionist (　　)
7. attention (　　)
8. avoid (　　)

a. a person that greets visitors to a company and answers the phone
b. to change the time or date of a planned event
c. you should listen because this is important
d. to take something and hold it
e. 100% correct
f. needing to be done now
g. to stay away from something
h. something you take when you are sick to make you better

# Listening Section

## PART 1　写真描写問題

 1-63,64

> ***Check Point!***　複数の人物の動作について述べるケースを見てましょう。
> Some people are opening the doors.

それぞれの写真について、4つの説明文の中から最も適切なものを1つずつ選びましょう。

1.

Ⓐ Ⓑ Ⓒ Ⓓ

2.
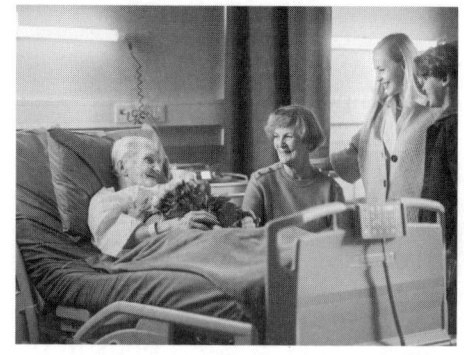
Ⓐ Ⓑ Ⓒ Ⓓ

## PART 2　応答問題

 1-65-69

> ***Check Point!***　頻出の疑問詞 How で始まる質問文を見てみましょう。
> How much exercise do you do a week?

それぞれの設問の応答として最も適切なものを1つずつ選びましょう。

**3.** Mark your answer on your answer sheet.　Ⓐ Ⓑ Ⓒ

**4.** Mark your answer on your answer sheet.　Ⓐ Ⓑ Ⓒ

**5.** Mark your answer on your answer sheet.　Ⓐ Ⓑ Ⓒ

**6.** Mark your answer on your answer sheet.　Ⓐ Ⓑ Ⓒ

**7.** Mark your answer on your answer sheet.　Ⓐ Ⓑ Ⓒ

## PART 3 会話問題  1-70,71

**Check Point!** 話し手の一方が何をしたいと言っているのか大きく捉えましょう。
What does the woman want to do?

会話についての設問に対し、最も適切なものを1つずつ選びましょう。

**8.** What will the woman do on Tuesday?
(A) Go to the doctor
(B) Go on a business trip
(C) Go to the library
(D) Go on vacation

**10.** Who most likely is the man?
(A) A doctor
(B) A patient
(C) A receptionist
(D) A travel agent

**9.** What does the woman want to do?
(A) Cancel a trip
(B) Change her doctor
(C) Reschedule her appointment
(D) See a doctor right away

## PART 4 説明文問題  1-72,73

**Check Point!** 告知を行っている話し手が誰かを聞き取りましょう。
Who is the speaker?

説明文についての設問に対し、最も適切なものを1つずつ選びましょう。

**11.** Who is the speaker?
(A) A gym member
(B) A fitness instructor
(C) A shop assistant
(D) A school teacher

**12.** What does the speaker say about next Monday?
(A) There will be a new class.
(B) There will be a new product.
(C) There will be a meeting.
(D) There will be some exciting news.

**13.** What does the speaker imply when she says, "so you don't miss it"?
(A) The sessions will be popular.
(B) The class will start very early.
(C) The trainer might not come.
(D) The class will be very difficult.

# ✍ Grammar Review 形容詞

■**形容詞**は名詞をより具体的に説明（修飾）するという大切な働きをしますが、その修飾の仕方には 3 パターンあることを覚えておきましょう。

① **名詞の前に置く**：You should eat **healthy** *food*.（健康的な食べ物）、のように修飾する名詞の前に置いて名詞の特徴や属性を説明するのが形容詞の最も一般的な使われ方です。

② **名詞の後ろに置く**：There was *only one room* **available** in the hospital.（1 部屋だけ空いている）と前の名詞を強調しています。名詞を後ろから修飾して名詞の性質や特性を具体的に説明するためにも使われます。*clothes* **suitable for exercise**（運動に適した服）。

③ **be 動詞の後ろに置く**：The air *is* **fresh**.（空気は新鮮だ）、では be 動詞の後ろに置いて補語として主語の The air を説明しています。

---

《例題》各空所に入れるべき最も適切な語句を 1 つ選んで、その記号を答えなさい。

1. Drinking enough water is ------- for staying healthy.
   (A) necessary　　(B) harmful　　(C) expensive　　(D) optional

2. The vegetables ------- in the market are fresh.
   (A) sell　　(B) sold　　(C) to be selling　　(D) to sell

---

# Reading Section

## ✅ 頻出単語チェック！ **Reading Section**

語句と意味を品詞に気をつけながら結びつけてみましょう。

1. frequent (　　)
2. suitable (　　)
3. skip [v.] (　　)
4. complete [v.] (　　)
5. concern [n.] (　　)
6. comfortable (　　)
7. reception (　　)
8. allowed (　　)

a. happening often
b. good for someone to use
c. something that you are worried about
d. to not go to something or not do something
e. relaxed and happy
f. to write all the information that is needed in a document
g. able to do something because the rules say it is OK
h. the place in a company where staff greet visitors and help them

## PART 5　短文穴埋め問題

**Check Point!**　文法問題：形容詞　語彙問題：副詞
形容詞は名詞や代名詞の前後に注目しましょう。

それぞれの空所に入れるのに最も適切なものを１つずつ選びましょう。

**14.** It's important to get ------- exercise in order to stay healthy.
(A) current
(B) frequent
(C) recent
(D) confident
Ⓐ Ⓑ Ⓒ Ⓓ

**15.** This medicine is not ------- for vegetarians.
(A) comfortable
(B) reasonable
(C) unable
(D) suitable
Ⓐ Ⓑ Ⓒ Ⓓ

**16.** Her usual doctor was away, so she made an appointment with a ------- doctor.
(A) different
(B) separate
(C) possible
(D) various
Ⓐ Ⓑ Ⓒ Ⓓ

**17.** Our baseball game finished ------- because it started to rain a lot.
(A) briefly
(B) fast
(C) early
(D) shortly
Ⓐ Ⓑ Ⓒ Ⓓ

**18.** I ------- skip my morning exercises, but today I was too busy.
(A) often
(B) rarely
(C) clearly
(D) carefully
Ⓐ Ⓑ Ⓒ Ⓓ

**Check Point!**　手紙　語彙問題：名詞、前置詞
文挿入問題：直前の文の流れに沿った自然な説明に注目しましょう。

それぞれの空所に入れるのに最も適切なものを1つずつ選びましょう。

---

Dr. F. Bernstein
St. Martin's Hospital
125 Main Street
Newtown

Dear Ms. White,

I am writing to confirm your ------- **19.** with Dr. Bernstein at St. Martin's Hospital at 2:00 P.M. on Tuesday, March 17.

Before your visit, please complete a form to tell us more about your health problems. ------- **20.** On the day of your visit, please bring it to the front desk.

If you have any questions or concerns ------- **21.** your visit, please feel free to contact me.

Sincerely,

Edward Fowler
Assistant to Dr. Bernstein

---

**19.** (A) appointment
(B) event
(C) calendar
(D) invitation

**21.** (A) by
(B) for
(C) to
(D) about

**20.** (A) This information is included on the form.
(B) You can find this form on our Web site.
(C) You should not write anything on this.
(D) Please ask Dr. Bernstein to give you one of these.

**PART 7** 読解問題

*Check Point!* 掲示（1つの文書、2つの質問）
質問が箇条書きのどの部分に該当するか見つけましょう

文章を読んで、それぞれの設問の答えとして最も適切なものを1つずつ選びましょう。

### Little Valley Sports Center Rules

1. Please do not eat anything in the sports center. You may take some water into the gym but this must be in a bottle.

2. Please do not talk on mobile phones inside the building. This includes the gym and the café. If you wish to talk on your phone, please go outside.

3. Please do not take any photographs inside the sports center. Other members may not be comfortable about being photographed.

4. Please do not use the machines without training from our staff. If you want training, please ask a member of staff at reception.

**22.** According to the notice, where can you use mobile phones?
   (A) Outside
   (B) In the gym
   (C) In the café
   (D) At reception

**23.** What is NOT mentioned in the notice?
   (A) Rules about where you can eat and drink
   (B) Reasons for not being allowed to take photos
   (C) Information on how to become a member
   (D) How to receive training for the machines

# UNIT 7 Purchasing

## :: *Warm up* — Dictation Practice  1-74

それぞれの空所に入る語を、音声を聞いて書き入れてみましょう。

1. Can you (　　　　　) (　　　　　) out?
2. (　　　　　) (　　　　　) get the receipt?
3. They asked (　　　　　) (　　　　　) quick delivery.
4. We'll (　　　　　) (　　　　　) today.
5. I'll take care (　　　　　) (　　　　　).
6. We're (　　　　　) (　　　　　) stock of that.
7. Let's look (　　　　　) (　　　　　) the options.
8. The prices (　　　　　) (　　　　　) this year.

### 🔍 Points to Dictate

前の語の最後の音が次の語の最初の音と連結するケースを練習しましょう。
2語ですが、まるで1語のように聞こえます。1語のように聞こえた瞬間に、
元の2語が思い浮かぶようになるのが目標です。

### ✔ 頻出単語チェック！ Listening Section

語句と意味を品詞に気をつけながら結びつけてみましょう。

1. try on (　　)
2. display [n.] (　　)
3. groceries (　　)
4. feature [n.] (　　)
5. occupied (　　)
6. taste [v.] (　　)
7. sign up (　　)
8. promote (　　)

a. to use advertisements to tell people about a product or service
b. to register for something
c. food that you buy from a supermarket
d. to have a flavor (e.g., sweet or salty)
e. some products put in the window of a store
f. an important part or characteristic of a product
g. to wear something to see if it looks and feels good
h. being used by someone else; full

 # Listening Section

> *Check Point!*  複数の人物全体、またはそのうちの1人の動作を見てみましょう。
> A woman is pushing a shopping cart.

それぞれの写真について、4つの説明文の中から最も適切なものを1つずつ選びましょう。

**1.**

Ⓐ Ⓑ Ⓒ Ⓓ

**2.**
Ⓐ Ⓑ Ⓒ Ⓓ

> *Check Point!*  頻出の疑問詞 What で始まる質問文を見てみましょう。
> What time does the store close?

それぞれの設問の応答として最も適切なものを1つずつ選びましょう。

**3.** Mark your answer on your answer sheet.  Ⓐ Ⓑ Ⓒ

**4.** Mark your answer on your answer sheet.  Ⓐ Ⓑ Ⓒ

**5.** Mark your answer on your answer sheet.  Ⓐ Ⓑ Ⓒ

**6.** Mark your answer on your answer sheet.  Ⓐ Ⓑ Ⓒ

**7.** Mark your answer on your answer sheet.  Ⓐ Ⓑ Ⓒ

*Check Point!* 話し手の一方が相手に何を依頼しているのか捉えましょう。
What does the woman ask the man to do?

会話についての設問に対し、最も適切なものを1つずつ選びましょう。

**8.** Where does the conversation most likely take place?
(A) In a restaurant
(B) In a hotel
(C) In a clothing store
(D) In a gym

**9.** What does the woman ask the man to do?
(A) Wait for the fitting room
(B) Try on the sweater
(C) Look for something
(D) Give her something

**10.** What does the woman offer to do?
(A) Give him a free item
(B) Find something for him
(C) Order another item
(D) Tell him when the room is ready

**PART 4**  説明文問題   1-84,85

*Check Point!* お知らせの目的は何か大きく捉えましょう。
What is the purpose of this announcement?

説明文についての設問に対し、最も適切なものを1つずつ選びましょう。

**11.** What is the purpose of this announcement?
(A) To thank customers
(B) To promote a product
(C) To apologize for a mistake
(D) To request some help

**12.** What does the speaker say about the new coffee?
(A) It is free if you have a store card.
(B) There is only one pack left.
(C) There is a special offer on it.
(D) It was made by a local coffee shop.

**13.** According to the speaker, what can shoppers get with a store card?
(A) Free samples
(B) Lower prices
(C) Cheap cups of coffee
(D) Special products

# 📀 Grammar Review 副詞

■**副詞**は動詞、形容詞、副詞を修飾する他、文全体を修飾します。

①**動詞を修飾する**：She **carefully** *checked* prices.（注意深く価格を*確認した*）

②**形容詞を修飾する**：His negotiation skills are **extremely** *good*.（非常に*優れている*）

③**副詞を修飾する**：She **very** *quickly* checked her e-mail.（とても*素早く*確認した）

careful+*ly*「注意深く」や usual+*ly*「通常」のように形容詞の語尾に接尾辞 -*ly* を付けて副詞を作ることが多いのですが、語尾が -ly でも lovely「素敵な」や silly「愚かな」のように副詞ではなく形容詞の単語もありますので注意しましょう。

さらに同じ単語が形容詞と副詞の両方の働きをするものがあります。The **fast** car is expensive.（速い車：形容詞）、She ran **fast** to ….（〜するために速く走った：副詞）

《例題》各空所に入れるべき最も適切な語を１つ選んで、その記号を答えなさい。

**1.** They ------- compare products before making a decision.

(A) careful　　(B) carefully　　(C) careless　　(D) caring

**2.** The jacket she bought was ------- cheap.

(A) surprisedly　　(B) surprising　　(C) surprisingly　　(D) surprises

 **Reading Section**

 ✔️ **頻出単語チェック！** **Reading Section**

語句と意味を品詞に気をつけながら結びつけてみましょう。

**1.** directions (　　)

**2.** review [n.] (　　)

**3.** attract (　　)

**4.** various (　　)

**5.** recent (　　)

**6.** in stock (　　)

**7.** supplier (　　)

**8.** apologies (　　)

**a.** the way to go to a place

**b.** in the store and ready for people to buy

**c.** someone's opinion of something (e.g., a movie or a restaurant)

**d.** saying that you are sorry about something

**e.** lots of different

**f.** to make people want to come to a place

**g.** happened not long ago

**h.** a company that provides a product or service for another company

それぞれの空所に入れるのに最も適切なものを1つずつ選びましょう。

**14.** This department store is becoming ------- busy since they reduced their prices.
    (A) increase
    (B) increased
    (C) increasing
    (D) increasingly      Ⓐ Ⓑ Ⓒ Ⓓ

**15.** After reading several reviews, she ------- decided to buy the new laptop.
    (A) final
    (B) finalize
    (C) finally
    (D) finalized      Ⓐ Ⓑ Ⓒ Ⓓ

**16.** They usually deliver items ------- fast, so we don't need to worry.
    (A) really
    (B) carefully
    (C) loudly
    (D) suddenly      Ⓐ Ⓑ Ⓒ Ⓓ

**17.** There was a 20% ------- on every item, so we bought a lot of things.
    (A) bargain
    (B) discount
    (C) deal
    (D) charge      Ⓐ Ⓑ Ⓒ Ⓓ

**18.** We asked one of the shop assistants for ------- to the toy department.
    (A) directions
    (B) destinations
    (C) instructions
    (D) locations      Ⓐ Ⓑ Ⓒ Ⓓ

## PART 6    長文穴埋め問題

それぞれの空所に入れるのに最も適切なものを1つずつ選びましょう。

---

### Book Fair This Weekend

Newtown's Summer Book Fair will be held in Washington Park this weekend. This event is ------- **19.** popular with local booksellers, but also attracts many used book stores from around the country area. You can find a lot of great books for very low prices.

As well as looking at the books, visitors can buy food and drink from various countries. ------- **20.** Here, they can play games and make their own books.

Last year, about 3,000 people came to the event and bought ------- **21.** 5,000 books.

---

**19.** (A) either
(B) neither
(C) both
(D) not only

**20.** (A) There is also a special area for children.
(B) This year, visitors can try Korean and Spanish food.
(C) There is a map of the park at the entrance.
(D) Local restaurants often bring food for people to try.

**21.** (A) above
(B) more
(C) over
(D) larger

文章を読んで、それぞれの設問の答えとして最も適切なものを１つずつ選びましょう。

## ✉ E-MAIL

| | |
|---|---|
| **To:** | Riku Kobayashi <r.kobayashi@tokyo-mail.com> |
| **From:** | Joan West <j.west@super-sports-store.com> |
| **Date:** | October 28 |
| **Subject:** | Information about your order |

Dear Mr. Kobayashi,

Thank you very much for your recent order. However, I am sorry to tell you that one of the items that you ordered cannot be sent this week. This is because of a problem with our online purchasing system.

The item that will be delayed is the red water bottle. Our online store showed that we had some in stock, but this was not correct. Some new stock will arrive from our supplier next month, so we will send your water bottle to you then. If you would prefer to cancel your order and get your money back for this item, please reply to this e-mail. All of the other items that you ordered will be delivered this week.

Please accept our apologies for this error.

Kind regards,

Joan West
Customer Service Assistant

**22.** What is the purpose of the e-mail?
(A) To confirm an order
(B) To request payment
(C) To explain a problem
(D) To cancel an item

**23.** What does Mr. Kobayashi need to do to cancel his order?
(A) Send a letter to the company
(B) Speak to the store manager
(C) Call customer service
(D) Reply to the e-mail

# UNIT 8 Personnel

**Warm up** — **Dictation Practice**  2-01

それぞれの空所に入る語を、音声を聞いて書き入れてみましょう。

1. We'll ( ) ( ) later.
2. I'll ( ) ( ) the new job.
3. I'll ( ) ( ) the application form.
4. We're looking ( ) ( ) the candidates.
5. Let's ( ) ( ) your work.
6. She's at the ( ) ( ) her field.
7. Let's ( ) ( ) a meeting tomorrow.
8. We're ( ) ( ) the new project.

---

🔍 **Points to Dictate**

引き続き、前の語の最後の音が次の語の最初の音と連結するケースを練習しましょう。1語のように聞こえた瞬間に元の2語が思い浮かぶようになるのが目標です。聞き取れた2語を1語であるかのように、自分で発話してみましょう。

---

✅ 頻出単語チェック！ **Listening Section**

語句と意味を品詞に気をつけながら結びつけてみましょう。

1. hand out [v.] ( )
2. seminar ( )
3. employee ( )
4. due ( )
5. identification card ( )
6. handle [v.] ( )
7. tip [n.] ( )
8. management ( )

a. a meeting where an expert and a group of people study something together
b. required to be done by a specific time
c. to give something (e.g., a document) to each member of a group
d. controlling something or someone
e. to be able to do something
f. a small piece of advice
g. a person that works for a company
h. an official card that shows a person's name and photograph

**PART 1** 写真描写問題  2-02,03

*Check Point!* 複数の人物全体、またはそのうちの1人の動作を見てみましょう。
Some people are talking to each other.

それぞれの写真について、4つの説明文の中から最も適切なものを1つずつ選びましょう。

1.

Ⓐ Ⓑ Ⓒ Ⓓ

2.

Ⓐ Ⓑ Ⓒ Ⓓ

**PART 2** 応答問題  2-04-08

*Check Point!* 助動詞shouldがさまざまな形で使われる質問文を見てみましょう。
Should I work late tonight?

それぞれの設問の応答として最も適切なものを1つずつ選びましょう。

**3.** Mark your answer on your answer sheet. Ⓐ Ⓑ Ⓒ

**4.** Mark your answer on your answer sheet. Ⓐ Ⓑ Ⓒ

**5.** Mark your answer on your answer sheet. Ⓐ Ⓑ Ⓒ

**6.** Mark your answer on your answer sheet. Ⓐ Ⓑ Ⓒ

**7.** Mark your answer on your answer sheet. Ⓐ Ⓑ Ⓒ

**PART 3**　会話問題　 2-09,10

*Check Point!*　話し手の2人が主に何について話しているか大きく捉えましょう。
What are the speakers mainly discussing?

会話についての設問に対し、最も適切なものを1つずつ選びましょう。

8. What are the speakers mainly discussing?
   (A) The woman's presentation
   (B) Advice about training
   (C) Tips for new managers
   (D) A trip to Chicago

9. What does the man suggest?
   (A) Including more tips
   (B) Providing more examples
   (C) Writing an e-mail
   (D) Attending the lesson

10. What will the woman most likely do next?
    (A) Visit Chicago
    (B) Ask for tips
    (C) Repeat the session
    (D) Change her presentation

**PART 4**　説明文問題　 2-11,12

*Check Point!*　話し手が誰であるか聞き取りましょう。
Who most likely is the speaker?

説明文についての設問に対し、最も適切なものを1つずつ選びましょう。

11. Who most likely is the speaker?
    (A) A business coach
    (B) An electrical engineer
    (C) A restaurant owner
    (D) A clothes designer

12. What does the woman mean when she says, "Well, you're not alone"?
    (A) She is reminding people to work together.
    (B) She is making the listeners feel better.
    (C) She is pleased to meet the listeners.
    (D) She is surprised at the number of people.

13. What will the speaker mainly talk about?
    (A) Job feedback
    (B) Overtime work rules
    (C) Tips for using technology
    (D) How to use time well

# Grammar Review 動名詞・不定詞・分詞-1（動名詞と不定詞）

■まず**動名詞・不定詞・分詞**の形を確認しておきましょう。

| 動名詞 | 不定詞 | 現在分詞 | 過去分詞 |
|---|---|---|---|
| ask*ing* | *to* ask | ask*ing* | ask*ed* |

動名詞は動詞の原形に -ing を、不定詞は to+ 動詞の原形、分詞では現在分詞（-ing）、過去分詞（-ed など）があります。動名詞と現在分詞は同じ形ですが、文中での役割が異なります。

【動名詞と不定詞の関係】

▶**名詞（句）としての働き**：動名詞と不定詞は名詞（句）を作って、文の主語や動詞の目的語として働きます。**Training** staff is important for every company.（社員研修は全ての企業にとって重要です）、**To hire** good staff is very important.（良いスタッフを採用することは非常に重要です）。どちらも be 動詞の前が文の主語です。両者は入れ換えが可能なこともありますが、動名詞が現在や過去の行為そのものを指し、to 不定詞はこれから起こる未来的な意味を持ち、目的や目標を指すという違いがあります。

---

《例題》各空所に入れるべき最も適切な語を 1 つ選んで、その記号を答えなさい。

**1.** ------- a friendly work environment increases job satisfaction.

    (A) Create    (B) Creates    (C) Created    (D) Creating

**2.** ------- the team is a manager's most important task.

    (A) To motivate    (B) Motivate    (C) Motivated    (D) Motivates

---

# Reading Section

## ✔ 頻出単語チェック！　Reading Section

単語と意味を品詞に気をつけながら結びつけてみましょう。

**1.** advertise (　　)    **a.** the cost of entrance to an event

**2.** trainer (　　)    **b.** to guide or direct a meeting or group

**3.** full-time [adj.] (　　)    **c.** a person who has finished their university education

**4.** lead [v.] (　　)    **d.** a chance to do or get something

**5.** opportunity (　　)    **e.** a person that teaches people how to do something

**6.** graduate [n.] (　　)    **f.** to use commercials or other advertisements to promote products or services

**7.** apply (　　)

**8.** admission (　　)    **g.** to officially request to get something (e.g., a job)

    **h.** working about seven hours a day over five days per week

## PART 5　短文穴埋め問題

**Check Point!**　文法問題：動名詞・不定詞・分詞-1（動名詞と不定詞）、語彙問題：動詞
動名詞や不定詞に注目し、文の主語や目的語に合わせましょう。

それぞれの空所に入れるのに最も適切なものを 1 つずつ選びましょう。

**14.** ------- a job in an online newspaper is pretty expensive.
(A) Advertise
(B) Advertised
(C) Advertises
(D) Advertising　　　　Ⓐ Ⓑ Ⓒ Ⓓ

**15.** ------- the best person for the job can take several months.
(A) Find
(B) Found
(C) Finding
(D) Finds　　　　Ⓐ Ⓑ Ⓒ Ⓓ

**16.** I believe that ------- people well, you need a lot of practice.
(A) interview
(B) interviews
(C) interviewed
(D) to interview　　　　Ⓐ Ⓑ Ⓒ Ⓓ

**17.** The company has finally ------- a new CEO after a six-month search.
(A) hired
(B) founded
(C) managed
(D) enclosed　　　　Ⓐ Ⓑ Ⓒ Ⓓ

**18.** Not many people wanted to join the class, so we decided to ------- it.
(A) cancel
(B) reserve
(C) enrol
(D) study　　　　Ⓐ Ⓑ Ⓒ Ⓓ

それぞれの空所に入れるのに最も適切なものを1つずつ選びましょう。

---

## Wanted: Business English Trainer

A large Japanese food company is hiring a business English trainer. The trainer ------- have five years of teaching experience, but does not need to speak Japanese.
**19.**

This is a full-time job at the company's office in Texas. The trainer will design and teach a training program to help Japanese sales staff talk to American customers. -------
**20.**

To -------, go to www.recruit-zone.com/jobs/pr-roles. For more details, contact greg@recruitzone.com
**21.**

---

**19.** (A) need
(B) might
(C) must
(D) would

**20.** (A) Also, he or she will learn different business skills.
(B) This course should be taught by the trainer.
(C) These customers need help with leading meetings.
(D) For example, the staff need to talk about products in English.

**21.** (A) apply
(B) application
(C) applicant
(D) applying

## PART 7　読解問題

文章を読んで、それぞれの設問の答えとして最も適切なものを1つずつ選びましょう。

---

### Looking for your first job?

Then come to the Young Person's Job Fair and find out about hundreds of exciting job opportunities! If you're graduating soon, this event is for you!

At the fair, you can meet staff from hundreds of big companies. They can tell you about jobs at their company and how you can apply. You can also watch several presentations about applying for jobs. Speakers will tell you how to read a job advertisement and how to write a good application. They will also give advice about job interviews.

The Young Person's Job Fair will be held at the Laketown Conference Center from July 19 to 21. Admission is free. Find out more at www.laketown-conferences.com/job-fair

---

**22.** Who most likely is the intended audience for the advertisement?
(A) Business owners
(B) High school teachers
(C) Staff at big companies
(D) University students

**23.** What does the advertisement indicate about the job fair?
(A) It does not cost anything.
(B) It lasts for a whole week.
(C) It will be held online.
(D) It is a very small event.

# UNIT 9 Corporate Development

## Warm up — Dictation Practice  2-13

それぞれの空所に入る語を、音声を聞いて書き入れてみましょう。

1. That's a (            ) (                    ) for a project.
2. Can you check (            ) (            ) ?
3. She looked (            ) (            ) closely.
4. We'll (            ) (            ) next week.
5. Please (            ) (            ) the light.
6. I'll (            ) (            ) done tomorrow.
7. I'll bring (            ) (            ) in the meeting.
8. We'll (            ) (            ) market this year.

### 🔍 Points to Dictate

引き続き、前の語の最後の音が次の語の最初の音と連結するケースを練習しましょう。1語のように聞こえた瞬間に元の2語が思い浮かぶようになるのが目標です。聞き取れた2語を1語であるかのように、自分で発話してみましょう。

### ✅ 頻出単語チェック！ Listening Section

単語と意味を品詞に気をつけながら結びつけてみましょう。

1. deadline [n.] (     )
2. impression (     )
3. instructions (     )
4. official [adj.] (     )
5. exciting (     )
6. accessory (     )
7. cover [n.] (     )
8. pharmacy (     )

a. making you feel happy and ready to do something
b. something that you put over or around something to protect it
c. an explanation of how to use or do something
d. an opinion of something or a feeling about it
e. something useful that you use with a machine
f. a shop that sells medicine
g. the date and/or time when something must be finished
h. agreed and approved by important people

# Listening Section

**PART 1** 写真描写問題  2-14,15

*Check Point!* 複数の人物の動作、もしくは複数の物の状態を見てみましょう。
People are sitting around a table.

それぞれの写真について、4つの説明文の中から最も適切なものを1つずつ選びましょう。

**1.**

Ⓐ Ⓑ Ⓒ Ⓓ

**2.**

Ⓐ Ⓑ Ⓒ Ⓓ

**PART 2** 応答問題  2-16-20

*Check Point!* 肯定形、否定形両方の平叙文に対する反応を選びましょう。
I can attend the meeting if you want.

それぞれの設問の応答として最も適切なものを1つずつ選びましょう。

**3.** Mark your answer on your answer sheet. Ⓐ Ⓑ Ⓒ

**4.** Mark your answer on your answer sheet. Ⓐ Ⓑ Ⓒ

**5.** Mark your answer on your answer sheet. Ⓐ Ⓑ Ⓒ

**6.** Mark your answer on your answer sheet. Ⓐ Ⓑ Ⓒ

**7.** Mark your answer on your answer sheet. Ⓐ Ⓑ Ⓒ

*Check Point!* 話し手の２人がどこで働いているか聞き取りましょう。
Where do the speakers most likely work?

会話についての設問に対し、最も適切なものを１つずつ選びましょう。

**8.** Where do the speakers most likely work?
(A) At a phone company
(B) At a supermarket
(C) At a newspaper
(D) At a design company

**9.** What will the woman do next week?
(A) Talk to some customers
(B) Creat a report
(C) Start selling the product
(D) Call the man

**10.** What does the woman suggest?
(A) Reducing the price
(B) Adding more colors
(C) Changing the size
(D) Making the instructions easier

*Check Point!* 話し手はどのような企業に勤めているのか聞き取りましょう。
What kind of business does the speaker work for?

説明文についての設問に対し、最も適切なものを１つずつ選びましょう。

**11.** What kind of business does the speaker work for?
(A) A fashion brand
(B) A pharmacy
(C) An electronics store
(D) A newsstand

**12.** Who most likely are the listeners?
(A) Journalists
(B) Staff
(C) Customers
(D) Designers

**13.** What does the man mean when he says, "it'll be official next week"?
(A) The new store will open.
(B) The price will go down.
(C) The deal will be announced.
(D) The new president will start.

## Grammar Review　動名詞・不定詞・分詞-2（不定詞と分詞）

【不定詞と分詞】

▶**形容詞（句）としての働き**：不定詞は形容詞（句）として名詞（句）を修飾することがありますが、分詞も同様の働きをします。不定詞は修飾する名詞（句）の直後に置かれることが多い一方、分詞は名詞（句）の直前にも直後にも置かれます。分詞が短い場合、a **growing** *company*（成長している会社）のように名詞の直前、分詞が長い場合、The *company* **growing rapidly**（急成長している会社）のように名詞の直後に来るというのが特徴です。また、このように分詞が -ing と現在分詞の場合「〜している」という能動の意味を表しますが、The *report* **written by the research team**（研究チームによって書かれた報告書）のように分詞が過去分詞の場合は「〜された」と受け身の意味を表します。

《例題》各空所に入れるべき最も適切な語句を１つ選んで、その記号を答えなさい。

1. The company needs a plan ------- in five years.
   (A) succeeds　　(B) succeeding　　(C) to succeed　　(D) succeed

2. The ------- economy is good news for business.
   (A) improving　　(B) improve　　(C) improves　　(D) improvement

3. The plan ------- by the team was successful.
   (A) create　　(B) created　　(C) creates　　(D) creating

## Reading Section

### ✔ 頻出単語チェック!　Reading Section

単語と意味を品詞に気をつけながら結びつけてみましょう。

1. conduct [v.] (　　)
2. proposal (　　)
3. potential [n.] (　　)
4. strategy (　　)
5. research [n.] (　　)
6. survey [n.] (　　)
7. quality (　　)
8. amount (　　)

a. studying something to learn more about it
b. a suggestion for a project
c. a plan to do something
d. a list of questions that you ask people to answer to get information
e. how much of something there is
f. to do something
g. how good (or bad) something is
h. the possibility of being successful in the future

> **Check Point!**
>
> 文法問題：動名詞・不定詞・分詞-2（不定詞と分詞）
> 語彙問題：名詞
> 修飾される名詞との位置関係に注意しましょう。

それぞれの空所に入れるのに最も適切なものを1つずつ選びましょう。

**14.** The research ------- by the marketing team in Brazil last month was really useful.
(A) conduct
(B) conducted
(C) conducting
(D) was conducted

Ⓐ Ⓑ Ⓒ Ⓓ

**15.** Our team needs a way ------- the costs of production.
(A) reduce
(B) reduces
(C) reducing
(D) to reduce

Ⓐ Ⓑ Ⓒ Ⓓ

**16.** Because of the ------- prices of materials, we have delayed the project.
(A) are increasing
(B) increase
(C) were increasing
(D) increasing

Ⓐ Ⓑ Ⓒ Ⓓ

**17.** The company announced a new ------- to expand its market overseas.
(A) strategy
(B) price
(C) profit
(D) payment

Ⓐ Ⓑ Ⓒ Ⓓ

**18.** Georgina presented her ------- to her manager and hoped that he would see the project's potential.
(A) approval
(B) warning
(C) proposal
(D) statement

Ⓐ Ⓑ Ⓒ Ⓓ

## PART 6　長文穴埋め問題

それぞれの空所に入れるのに最も適切なものを１つずつ選びましょう。

---

### About us

Happy Jacks has made toys for children for more than 50 years. Our owner Jack Monroe was a furniture maker. He loved making things --------- wood, so he **19.** decided to try making some toys.

At first, it was just fun to do, but people loved his toys, and he was soon selling more toys than furniture. --------- **20.**

The shop was a big success, so five years later Jack opened an online store. Now even more children can enjoy --------- with his toys. **21.**

---

**19.** (A) by
　　 (B) with
　　 (C) as
　　 (D) for

**20.** (A) But he made more furniture.
　　 (B) But he didn't make much money.
　　 (C) So he stopped making toys.
　　 (D) So he opened a toy shop.

**21.** (A) play
　　 (B) plays
　　 (C) playing
　　 (D) played

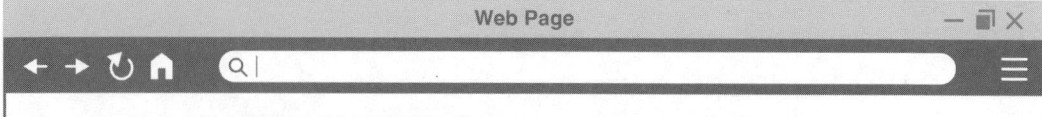

**Check Point!** ウェブページ（1つの文書、2つの質問）
調査ではどのような結果が得られたのか読み取りましょう。

文章を読んで、それぞれの設問の答えとして最も適切なものを1つずつ選びましょう。

---

**Web Page** — ▢ ×

Q |

### COMPANY NEWS: Customer Research Results

The sales team did some research on customers' opinions of our shampoo. The team conducted a survey and then spoke to more than fifty customers at stores that sell our products.

The main results were that customers are happy with the quality of our products, but they want to be able to buy them in larger amounts. Our bottles are 200 ml, but most customers say they would prefer to buy a 400-ml or 500-ml bottle.

The most popular product was our lemon shampoo. Many customers said it really helped them to wake up in the morning. However, our peach shampoo was less popular and some people said it made their hair feel dry.

Most customers said they are interested in trying an orange shampoo, but they are not interested in strawberry.

---

**22.** According to the Web page, what is true about the company's lemon shampoo?
   (A) It makes customers' hair feel bad.
   (B) It is only sold in large bottles right now.
   (C) It is most customers' favorite shampoo.
   (D) It will be changed to an orange shampoo.

**23.** What will most likely happen next?
   (A) The company will make strawberry shampoo.
   (B) The company will make bigger bottles of shampoo.
   (C) The sales team will talk to more customers.
   (D) The sales team will make a new survey.

# UNIT 10 Entertainment

## Warm up　　　Dictation Practice　　 2-25

それぞれの空所に入る語を、音声を聞いて書き入れてみましょう。

1. I don't know (　　　　　　) that movie.
2. I don't know (　　　　　　) when the show starts.
3. We'll meet (　　　　　) the theater.
4. I really (　　　　　) your help with this event.
5. Did you bring your (　　　　　)?
6. I (　　　　　) it to be fun.
7. I can't (　　　　　) we got tickets.
8. The show starts at (　　　　　) past eight.

---

### 🔍 Points to Dictate

発話されると単語の中のある音が消えてしまうことがあります。例えば about は abóut と ó にストレスがあるため、始めの a が消えて /bóut/ のように発話されます。単語のストレスが置かれる場所との関係で起こる 「音の消失」。何の音が消えているのか意識しましょう。

---

### ✔ 頻出単語チェック！ Listening Section

語句と意味を品詞に気をつけながら結びつけてみましょう。

1. hang (　　)
2. remove (　　)
3. pick up (　　)
4. booking (　　)
5. row [n.] (　　)
6. talented (　　)
7. gallery (　　)
8. exhibition (　　)

a. highly skilled
b. a reservation
c. to go somewhere by car to get someone
d. a line of seats in a theater
e. a building where people look at paintings and artwork
f. a collection of artwork with a connection (e.g., all by the same painter)
g. to take something away
h. to fix a picture to a wall

# Listening Section

## PART 1 写真描写問題

 2-26,27

*Check Point!* 複数の人物の動作、もしくは複数の物の状態を見てみましょう。
Some boats are in the river.

それぞれの写真について、4つの説明文の中から最も適切なものを1つずつ選びましょう。

1.

2.

Ⓐ Ⓑ Ⓒ Ⓓ    Ⓐ Ⓑ Ⓒ Ⓓ

## PART 2 応答問題

 2-28-32

*Check Point!* 助動詞 Would で始まる疑問文には提案や丁寧な依頼の意味もあります。
Would you help me with this report?

それぞれの設問の応答として最も適切なものを1つずつ選びましょう。

**3.** Mark your answer on your answer sheet.　　Ⓐ Ⓑ Ⓒ

**4.** Mark your answer on your answer sheet.　　Ⓐ Ⓑ Ⓒ

**5.** Mark your answer on your answer sheet.　　Ⓐ Ⓑ Ⓒ

**6.** Mark your answer on your answer sheet.　　Ⓐ Ⓑ Ⓒ

**7.** Mark your answer on your answer sheet.　　Ⓐ Ⓑ Ⓒ

## PART 3 会話問題

2-33,34

***Check Point!*** 話し手の一方がなぜ電話しているのか聞き取りましょう。
Why is the man calling?

会話についての設問に対し、最も適切なものを1つずつ選びましょう。

**8.** Why is the man calling?
(A) To ask about prices
(B) To cancel a booking
(C) To change a booking
(D) To check some information

**9.** What does the woman mean when she says, "I can move your seats"?
(A) She can change the time.
(B) She can give them different seats.
(C) She can change the day.
(D) She can cancel their tickets.

**10.** Where will they sit?
(A) Near the front
(B) Near the back
(C) In the middle
(D) On the balcony

## PART 4 説明文問題

2-35,36

***Check Point!*** どのような宣伝が行われているのか聞き取りましょう。
What is being advertised?

説明文についての設問に対し、最も適切なものを1つずつ選びましょう。

**11.** What is being advertised?
(A) An art gallery
(B) An art shop
(C) A lecture about art
(D) A painting course

**12.** Who is Norman James?
(A) A museum worker
(B) A local artist
(C) A paint shop owner
(D) A student

**13.** What will happen next week?
(A) A course will start.
(B) An exhibition will start.
(C) People can sign up.
(D) Paints can be bought.

# Grammar Review 動名詞・不定詞・分詞-3（不定詞と分詞構文）

【不定詞と分詞構文】

▶**副詞（句）としての働き**：不定詞は文の中で副詞（句）として働き、「目的」や「結果」を表します。He stayed up late **to watch his favorite movie**. では不定詞句の to watch his favorite movie は「お気に入りの映画を見るために」という目的を表しています。

分詞もまた、分詞構文の形で文に情報を補足する働きを持っています。**Excited by the concert**, she danced along with the music. では分詞が「コンサートに興奮して」と、彼女が音楽に合わせて踊った理由を補足しています。**Sitting by the fire**, he played the guitar. では「火のそばに座って」と、彼がギターを弾いた状況を補足しています。分詞構文は文の補足情報で、文の要点とは別なのでカンマで区切ります。

《例題》各空所に入れるべき最も適切な語を1つ選んで、その記号を答えなさい。

1. They brought a camera ------- photos.
   (A) takes　　(B) taking　　(C) taken　　(D) to take

2. ------- by the movie, he forgot the time.
   (A) Fascinate　　(B) Fascinated　　(C) Fascinating　　(D) To fascinate

3. ------- in the park, they played cards together.
   (A) Sit　　(B) Sits　　(C) Sitting　　(D) Sat

# Reading Section

## ☑ 頻出単語チェック！　Reading Section

語句と意味を品詞に気をつけながら結びつけてみましょう。

1. confident (　　)
2. noise (　　)
3. history (　　)
4. item (　　)
5. cover [v.] (　　)
6. details (　　)
7. catch [v.] (　　)
8. look around (　　)

a. sure that you will be successful
b. to include in a presentation, book, essay, etc.
c. to get a train, bus, boat, or plane
d. a loud sound
e. information about something or someone
f. an object; a thing
g. the study of the past
h. to go somewhere and look at many things there

**PART 5** 短文穴埋め問題

**Check Point!**

文法問題：動名詞・不定詞・分詞-3（不定詞と分詞構文）
語彙問題：形容詞
分詞構文では主節と分詞構文の主語が一致しているか確認しましょう。

それぞれの空所に入れるのに最も適切なものを 1 つずつ選びましょう。

14. ------- at the prices of the tickets, they decided not to go to the concert.
    (A) Surprising
    (B) Surprise
    (C) Surprised
    (D) To surprise                        Ⓐ Ⓑ Ⓒ Ⓓ

15. They went to the gallery ------- the show before it finished.
    (A) seeing
    (B) see
    (C) saw
    (D) to see                             Ⓐ Ⓑ Ⓒ Ⓓ

16. ------- to the music, she thought about her trip to South America.
    (A) Listen
    (B) Listened
    (C) Listening
    (D) To listen                          Ⓐ Ⓑ Ⓒ Ⓓ

17. Before he started to sing, Elliot always felt very ------- about making a mistake.
    (A) safe
    (B) confident
    (C) worried
    (D) bored                              Ⓐ Ⓑ Ⓒ Ⓓ

18. The noise at the concert was so ------- that I decided to leave.
    (A) loud
    (B) large
    (C) various
    (D) hard                               Ⓐ Ⓑ Ⓒ Ⓓ

それぞれの空所に入れるのに最も適切なものを1つずつ選びましょう。

---

## Learn about the History of our City

The City Museum Director, Laura Young, will give several talks about the history of Manchester over the next six months. In ------- talk, she will use items from
**19.**
the museum to tell the story of our city.

The first talk will be about the early days of Manchester. ------- She will also talk
**20.**
about the first people who lived here. In future talks, she will discuss the biggest events in our history, important buildings in the city, and people's jobs in the city one hundred years -------.
**21.**

For more details, see www.manchester-museum.com/talks

---

**19.** (A) some
(B) all
(C) the
(D) each

**20.** (A) It will cover the most recent history of the city.
(B) Some of these people became very famous.
(C) Ms. Young will explain how the city was built.
(D) Who built the city and who were the first people to live here?

**21.** (A) before
(B) ago
(C) last
(D) later

*Check Point!* テキストメッセージ（1つの文書、2つの質問）
2人は何時にどこで会うことになったのか注目しましょう。

文章を読んで、それぞれの設問の答えとして最も適切なものを1つずつ選びましょう。

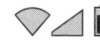

| Leonard | 3:03 P.M. |
| --- | --- |
| What time shall we meet on Sunday? | |

| Amy | 3:04 P.M. |
| --- | --- |
| Well, the concert starts at 7:00, so how about we get the train at 6:00? | |

| Leonard | 3:05 P.M. |
| --- | --- |
| Actually, can we go a little earlier? The trains are probably going to be really busy. | |

| Amy | 3:05 P.M. |
| --- | --- |
| Good point. What about 5:00 then? Perhaps we can eat something near the stadium. | |

| Leonard | 3:06 P.M. |
| --- | --- |
| Yeah, there are lots of restaurants and cafés around there. | |

| Amy | 3:07 P.M. |
| --- | --- |
| I think there's a train at 4:50. Can you catch that one? | |

| Leonard | 3:07 P.M. |
| --- | --- |
| Sure. I can get to the station at 4:40. Meet you near the entrance? | |

| Amy | 3:08 P.M. |
| --- | --- |
| Sounds good. I'll probably get there at about 4:20 because I want to look around the shops first, so I'll be waiting for you! | |

| Leonard | 3:08 P.M. |
| --- | --- |
| OK! | |

**22.** What time are they going to meet?
   (A) 4:20 P.M.
   (B) 4:40 P.M.
   (C) 4:50 P.M.
   (D) 5:00 P.M.

**23.** Where will Amy and Leonard meet?
   (A) At the stadium
   (B) On the train
   (C) At the station
   (D) At a shop

# Technical Areas

**Dictation Practice**  2-37

それぞれの空所に入る語を、音声を聞いて書き入れてみましょう。

**1.** They can't (　　　　　　　) the error.
**2.** We need to repair it (　　　　　　　) it's important.
**3.** The test will take (　　　　　　) minutes.
**4.** It's an (　　　　　　) conference.
**5.** The display looks (　　　　　　) now.
**6.** We need to (　　　　　　) using the new tool.
**7.** The machine (　　　　　) stopped.
**8.** It's an (　　　　　　) problem to solve.

**🔍 Points to Dictate**

引き続き、「音の消失」するケースを練習しましょう。ストレスの位置を思い浮かべながら、どの音が消えているのか、消えた音が何かをすぐに判別できるようになるのが目標です。

**✔️ 頻出単語チェック！** **Listening Section**

語句と意味を品詞に気をつけながら結びつけてみましょう。

**1.** mouse (　　)
**2.** rack [n.] (　　)
**3.** set up (　　)
**4.** equipment (　　)
**5.** compare (　　)
**6.** cable (　　)
**7.** patience (　　)
**8.** repairs (　　)

**a.** working to mend something that is broken
**b.** a wire; used to connect a machine to power or to connect two machines
**c.** machines, tools, and other things needed for a special purpose
**d.** to get something ready to be used
**e.** the ability to wait without getting annoyed
**f.** a machine that helps you to use a computer
**g.** a bar or a set of bars for holding things
**h.** to look for similarities and differences between two or more things

**Listening Section**

## PART 1　写真描写問題  2-38,39

**Check Point!**　特定の人物の動作、もしくは複数の物の状態を見てみましょう。
The woman is using a mouse.

それぞれの写真について、4つの説明文の中から最も適切なものを1つずつ選びましょう。

1.

Ⓐ Ⓑ Ⓒ Ⓓ

2.

Ⓐ Ⓑ Ⓒ Ⓓ

## PART 2　応答問題  2-40-44

**Check Point!**　助動詞としてのDoを使ったさまざまな疑問文を見てみましょう。
Do you know the head of the IT department?

それぞれの設問の応答として最も適切なものを1つずつ選びましょう。

**3.** Mark your answer on your answer sheet. Ⓐ Ⓑ Ⓒ

**4.** Mark your answer on your answer sheet. Ⓐ Ⓑ Ⓒ

**5.** Mark your answer on your answer sheet. Ⓐ Ⓑ Ⓒ

**6.** Mark your answer on your answer sheet. Ⓐ Ⓑ Ⓒ

**7.** Mark your answer on your answer sheet. Ⓐ Ⓑ Ⓒ

 **PART 3** 会話問題  2-45,46

*Check Point!* 話し手の一方がどこで働いているか聞き取りましょう。
Where does the woman most likely work?

会話についての設問に対し、最も適切なものを1つずつ選びましょう。

8. Where does the woman most likely
   work?
   (A) At a printing company
   (B) At a computer company
   (C) At an electronics store
   (D) At a photo studio

9. What does the woman say about
   the printer?
   (A) It only prints photographs.
   (B) It's very expensive.
   (C) It's perfect for the office.
   (D) It's a new product.

10. What will the man probably do
    next?
    (A) Print some photographs
    (B) Purchase the printer
    (C) Leave the store
    (D) Compare different models

**PART 4** 説明文問題  4-47,48

*Check Point!* どのような問題が述べられているのか聞き取りましょう。
What problem does the speaker mention?

説明文についての設問に対し、最も適切なものを1つずつ選びましょう。

11. What problem does the speaker
    mention?
    (A) The company's Web site is not
        working.
    (B) The company's phones are not
        working.
    (C) Some customers' Internet is not
        working.
    (D) Some customers' cable TV is not
        working.

12. What caused the problem?
    (A) Too many customers were using
        the service.
    (B) They were using some old
        cables.
    (C) There was some bad weather
        yesterday.
    (D) They do not have enough
        engineers.

13. When will the repairs be completed?
    (A) In the next 12 hours
    (B) In the next couple of hours
    (C) In the next week
    (D) In the next day

# ⚡ Grammar Review　前置詞

■**前置詞**は、文の中で場所や時間などの情報を追加するために使われる言葉です。前置詞は名詞や代名詞の前に置かれます。前置詞の後に来る名詞や代名詞は「前置詞の目的語」と呼ばれます。「前置詞＋名詞」の組み合わせは「前置詞句」と呼ばれ、前置詞句は、形容詞のように名詞を説明したり、副詞のように動詞を説明したりします。

1. Look at the *picture* **on the wall.**（壁の絵を見なさい）では picture を修飾する形容詞句。
2. Did you *put* the picture **on the wall**?（壁に絵を掛けたか）では動詞 put を修飾する副詞句。

▶**時間に関する**代表的な前置詞には at, in, on があります。at は at one（1 時）や at noon（正午）のようにピンポイントの一時を指すイメージです。in は in March（3 月）や in spring（春）のように長い期間を指すときに使われます。on は at と in の中間で on Sunday（日曜日）や on May 17（5 月 17 日）のように使われます。

---

《例題》各空所に入れるべき最も適切な語を 1 つ選んで、その記号を答えなさい。

**1.** We plan to install new software on the computers ------- December.
(A) while　　(B) on　　(C) at　　(D) in

**2.** The engineering project starts ------- 10:00 A.M. tomorrow.
(A) at　　(B) in　　(C) on　　(D) for

---

# 📖 Reading Section

## ✅ 頻出単語チェック！ **Reading Section**

語句と意味を品詞に気をつけながら結びつけてみましょう。

1. pick up (　　)
2. distribute (　　)
3. fix [v.] (　　)
4. unfortunately (　　)
5. available (　　)
6. look forward to (　　)
7. security (　　)
8. protect (　　)

**a.** to make something broken work again
**b.** sadly; unluckily
**c.** not busy or being used by someone
**d.** to share things out between several people
**e.** to feel happy or excited about something that will happen in the future
**f.** to collect something from somewhere
**g.** to stop something from being damaged or stolen
**h.** keeping someone or something safe from crime and danger

## PART 5 短文穴埋め問題

**Check Point!**

文法問題：前置詞　語彙問題：動詞
時間や場所などそれぞれに合った前置詞を選びましょう。

それぞれの空所に入れるのに最も適切なものを1つずつ選びましょう。

**14.** The company has decided to start using new software ------- April next year.
(A) at
(B) in
(C) on
(D) to　　　　　　　　　　　　　　　　Ⓐ Ⓑ Ⓒ Ⓓ

**15.** I plan to go to a technology conference in Paris ------- Thursday next week.
(A) at
(B) in
(C) on
(D) to　　　　　　　　　　　　　　　　Ⓐ Ⓑ Ⓒ Ⓓ

**16.** Please come to the office ------- 11 o'clock tomorrow to pick up your computer.
(A) at
(B) in
(C) on
(D) for　　　　　　　　　　　　　　　　Ⓐ Ⓑ Ⓒ Ⓓ

**17.** The company has decided to ------- some money in better computer systems.
(A) acquire
(B) consume
(C) invest
(D) purchase　　　　　　　　　　　　　　Ⓐ Ⓑ Ⓒ Ⓓ

**18.** After today's meeting, Laura will ------- the training materials to all staff.
(A) arrange
(B) distribute
(C) possess
(D) require　　　　　　　　　　　　　　Ⓐ Ⓑ Ⓒ Ⓓ

それぞれの空所に入れるのに最も適切なものを１つずつ選びましょう。

---

**To:** William Brown <w.brown@southern-travel.com>
**From:** Kate Carter <k.carter@color-printer-co.com>
**Subject:** Re: Printer problem
**Date:** April 24

---

Dear Mr. Brown,

We are very sorry to hear that you are having problems with your printer. We
-------- be happy to send an engineer to your office to check the problem and
**19.**
fix it.

Unfortunately, all of our engineers are busy tomorrow, but we can send
someone to your office the day after tomorrow. -------- If you are not available
**20.**
then, please contact me and let me know the best day and time for you.

Once again, -------- apologize for the problems that you are having.
**21.**

Kind regards,

Kate Carter
Color Printer Co.

19. (A) could
    (B) might
    (C) should
    (D) would

20. (A) So, I set the visit for 10:00 A.M. on that day.
    (B) So please tell me when would be a good day for you.
    (C) I hope that this is not too early in the morning for you.
    (D) We are all really looking forward to your visit.

21. (A) we
    (B) our
    (C) you
    (D) your

**Check Point!**
Ｅメールと申請書（２つの文書、３つの質問）
Ｅメールの目的と何の申請書かに注目しましょう。

文章を読んで、それぞれの設問の答えとして最も適切なものを１つずつ選びましょう。

---

### ✉ E-MAIL

| | |
|---|---|
| **To:** | Louisa Gray |
| **From:** | Sandra Johnson |
| **Date:** | April 17 |
| **Subject:** | Applying for a Staff ID Card |

Hi Louisa,

Welcome to The Green Energy Company!

I am writing to explain how you can get your staff ID card. It's important that you do this as soon as possible so that you can move freely around the building. We are very careful about security in this building to protect our technology. Without an ID card, you must be with another member of staff whenever you go somewhere.

To get your ID card, please fill out the Staff ID Card Application Form and bring it to the reception desk. Also, please bring some other ID, such as a driver's license or passport. We will take a photograph of you and create your card for you.

The reception desk is on the first floor.

Kind regards,

Sandra

---

### STAFF ID CARD APPLICATION FORM

| | |
|---|---|
| **Name:** | Louisa Gray |
| **Department:** | Customer Service |
| **Manager:** | Matthew Connor |
| **Start date:** | April 17 |
| **Staff ID no:** | 000982 |
| **Method of travel:** | Subway |

**To be completed by security staff**

☐ ID checked
☐ Photograph taken
☐ Card supplied

**22.** What is the purpose of the e-mail?
   (A) To welcome someone
   (B) To warn someone
   (C) To make a request
   (D) To provide instructions

**23.** What does Ms. Johnson ask Ms. Gray to do?
   (A) Take a photograph of herself
   (B) Send the form by e-mail
   (C) Tell her manager to fill out the form
   (D) Show some ID at the reception desk

**24.** What is indicated about Ms. Gray
   (A) She has just joined the company.
   (B) She is visiting the company.
   (C) She works at the reception desk.
   (D) She plans to drive to work.

# UNIT
## 12

# Offices

**Dictation Practice**  2-49

それぞれの空所に入る語を、音声を聞いて書き入れてみましょう。

1. She ( ) ( ) work in this office.
2. I'm ( ) ( ) call him later.
3. He ( ) ( ) talk about the project.
4. ( ) ( ) your plans for today?
5. ( ) ( ) you think about this idea?
6. ( ) ( ) down and discuss this.
7. We ( ) ( ) make a decision soon.
8. ( ) ( ), I'll be there.

**Points to Dictate**

ある音が隣の音の影響を受けて、その音に似たり、同じ音になったりすることが起こります。例えば、of の /f/ は単独では / ヴ / と発音されますが of+course の連結で見ると course の最初の子音 /c/ に影響され / オフ / と変化、/ オフコース / となります。

**✓ 頻出単語チェック！** **Listening Section**

単語と意味を品詞に気をつけながら結びつけてみましょう。

1. shelf ( )
2. pile [n.] ( )
3. drawer ( )
4. cabinet ( )
5. notify ( )
6. fit [v.] ( )
7. mention [v.] ( )
8. install ( )

a. to put some software onto a computer
b. part of some furniture that can be opened so things can be put inside
c. a tall piece of furniture where things can be kept
d. a flat board to put things (e.g., books)
e. to talk about something – often just for a short time without giving much detail
f. to be able to put something in a place because there is space
g. many things on top of each other
h. to tell someone something in an official way

 **Listening Section**

## PART 1    写真描写問題    2-50,51

**Check Point!**

1つまたは複数の物の状態について述べるケースを見てみましょう。

There is a printer on the floor.

それぞれの写真について、4つの説明文の中から最も適切なものを1つずつ選びましょう。

**1.**

Ⓐ Ⓑ Ⓒ Ⓓ

**2.**

Ⓐ Ⓑ Ⓒ Ⓓ

## PART 2    応答問題    2-52-56

**Check Point!**

助動詞 Can と Could を使った疑問文は「依頼・許可」を表します。

Can you tell me where the kitchen is?

それぞれの設問の応答として最も適切なものを1つずつ選びましょう。

**3.** Mark your answer on your answer sheet.    Ⓐ Ⓑ Ⓒ

**4.** Mark your answer on your answer sheet.    Ⓐ Ⓑ Ⓒ

**5.** Mark your answer on your answer sheet.    Ⓐ Ⓑ Ⓒ

**6.** Mark your answer on your answer sheet.    Ⓐ Ⓑ Ⓒ

**7.** Mark your answer on your answer sheet.    Ⓐ Ⓑ Ⓒ

> ***Check Point!***  会話がどこで行われているか大きく捉えましょう。
> Where does the conversation most likely take place?

会話についての設問に対し、最も適切なものを1つずつ選びましょう。

**8.** Where does the conversation most likely take place?
(A) In a kitchen
(B) In a meeting room
(C) In a laboratory
(D) In a storage room

**9.** According to the man, what will the company do next month?
(A) Move the table
(B) Buy some furniture
(C) Paint the room
(D) Begin to use the room

**10.** What does the man suggest?
(A) Choosing leather chairs
(B) Finding a new meeting room
(C) Removing some chairs
(D) Changing the table size

**PART 4**  説明文問題   2-59,60

> ***Check Point!***  話し手が電話している理由を聞き取りましょう。
> Why is the woman calling?

説明文についての設問に対し、最も適切なものを1つずつ選びましょう。

**11.** Why is the woman calling?
(A) To ask a question about some software
(B) To order some new equipment
(C) To arrange to repair something
(D) To help with a problem

**12.** What does the speaker mean when she says, "I'll set up the new one"?
(A) I'll leave a new computer for you to pick up.
(B) I'll order a new computer for you.
(C) I'll get a new computer ready for you.
(D) I'll repair your new computer for you.

**13.** What will the listener most likely do next?
(A) Come into the office
(B) Purchase a new laptop
(C) Install some special software
(D) Suggest a meeting time

## 🎯 Grammar Review 接続詞

■**接続詞**には**等位接続詞**と**従属接続詞**の２種類があります。**等位接続詞**は接続詞を挟んで文と文、節と節、句と句を対等に結びつけます。The meeting room is *large* **and** *quiet*.（会議室は広くて静かだ）。等位接続詞には for, and, nor, but, or, yet, so の７つがあります。

**従属接続詞**は主節に情報を補足的に加えるための接続詞です。補足情報を含む節を従属節と言います。You can't enter the office ***unless*** *you have a key.*（鍵を持っていなければオフィスに入ることができない）。unless 以下の従属節が情報を補足しています。従属接続詞は 1. 条件（if, unless など）、2. 譲歩（though, although など）、3. 原因・理由（because, since など）、4. 目的（so that ～など）5. 時（when, before など）6. 様態（as, like など）7. 制限・範囲（as long as..., as far as...）8. 結果・程度（so ＋形容詞［副詞］＋ that...）と８つあります。

《例題》各空所に入れるべき最も適切な語を１つ選んで、その記号を答えなさい。

**1.** We have new desks ------- comfortable chairs in the office.
(A) or　　(B) but　　(C) and　　(D) so

**2.** She answers calls ------- it's her job.
(A) unless　　(B) before　　(C) although　　(D) because

**3.** Turn off all the lights ------- leaving the office.
(A) before　　(B) but　　(C) though　　(D) since

## Reading Section

### ✅ 頻出単語チェック！ Reading Section

単語と意味を品詞に気をつけながら結びつけてみましょう。

**1.** empty [adj.] (　　)　　　**a.** a person who cleans rooms in a house or office for their job
**2.** task [n.] (　　)
**3.** transportation (　　)　　**b.** doing the things you have been asked to do
**4.** slightly (　　)　　　　**c.** a little
**5.** latest (　　)　　　　　**d.** not containing anything
**6.** expect (　　)　　　　　**e.** newest
**7.** cleaner [n.] (　　)　　　**f.** e.g., cars, buses, trains, and planes
**8.** cooperation (　　)　　　**g.** a piece of work that needs to be done
　　　　　　　　　　　　　**h.** to think that something will happen

それぞれの空所に入れるのに最も適切なものを1つずつ選びましょう。

**14.** Our office is on the first floor, ------- I never take the elevator.
(A) but
(B) for
(C) so
(D) yet

Ⓐ Ⓑ Ⓒ Ⓓ

**15.** ------- we have ten meeting rooms in our office, it's often hard to find an empty one.
(A) Although
(B) After
(C) Before
(D) Unless

Ⓐ Ⓑ Ⓒ Ⓓ

**16.** You can take a day off tomorrow ------- your tasks are completed.
(A) although
(B) if
(C) where
(D) unless

Ⓐ Ⓑ Ⓒ Ⓓ

**17.** Our manager will share the new ------- for the project.
(A) schedule
(B) performance
(C) delivery
(D) ticket

Ⓐ Ⓑ Ⓒ Ⓓ

**18.** The company will pay for ------- to work for all staff starting next month.
(A) operation
(B) communication
(C) education
(D) transportation

Ⓐ Ⓑ Ⓒ Ⓓ

**PART 6** 長文穴埋め問題

*Check Point!* メモ 文法問題：語形選択
文挿入問題：理由や結果の説明が自然に続くかを確認しましょう。

それぞれの空所に入れるのに最も適切なものを１つずつ選びましょう。

---

**Memo**

**About Our August Meeting**

1. Helen told us the ----19.---- information about our two current projects. The Web site for Shaw and Co. is still in the planning stage, but we had a good meeting with them last week. Also, we have finished ----20.---- the design for the Web site for Murdoch Inc. It should be ready by the end of the month.

2. Brenda told us that finding a new designer is taking longer than expected. She thinks the salary that we offered is too low. ----21.---- So, we will try another advertisement with a slightly higher salary.

---

**19.** (A) late
(B) later
(C) latest
(D) lately

**20.** (A) mostly
(B) most of
(C) almost
(D) most

**21.** (A) That's why only people with not much experience are applying.
(B) This is why so many people have applied.
(C) But we cannot pay a higher salary to the designer.
(D) We've decided to stop trying to find someone.

*Check Point!*    メモとEメール（2つの文書、3つの質問）
メモの目的と社員の行動についての内容に注目しましょう。

文章を読んで、それぞれの設問の答えとして最も適切なものを1つずつ選びましょう。

---

## Memo: A Cleaner Office

Dear Team,

Starting next week, we will have some new office cleaners. [1] They will come on Monday, Wednesday, and Friday at 6 P.M. [2] On these days, please remove all items from your desk before leaving. Do not leave any empty cups, cans or bottles on your desk. Also, please put all papers and personal items in your drawers. [3] A clean office not only looks nicer, but also helps us to do our work better.

Thank you for your cooperation. If you have any questions, please let me know by e-mail. [4]

Best regards,

John Davis
Office Management

## ✉ E-MAIL

| From: | Barbara Williams |
| --- | --- |
| To: | John Davis |
| Date: | May 19 |
| Subject: | Question About the New Cleaners |

Dear John,

I understand that new cleaners will come to the office in the evenings. Sometimes I stay late for online meetings with overseas customers. I'm worried the cleaners will be noisy. When can I have my meetings? As you know, I don't work on Tuesdays.

Thanks for your help!

Kind regards,

Barbara Williams

---

**22.** What is the purpose of the memo?
(A) To explain about office cleaning
(B) To remind staff about a deadline
(C) To announce a new project
(D) To advertise some new jobs

**23.** In which of the positions marked [1], [2], [3], and [4] does the following sentence best belong?
"These small actions will help the cleaners to do their job more easily."
(A) [1]
(B) [2]
(C) [3]
(D) [4]

**24.** What day will Ms. Williams most likely have her meetings?
(A) Monday
(B) Tuesday
(C) Wednesday
(D) Thursday

# UNIT 13 Travel

それぞれの空所に入る語を、音声を聞いて書き入れてみましょう。

**John:** Are you ready to ¹(      ) (      ) the airport?

**Karen:** Yes, almost, but I ²(      ) (      ) my coffee yet.

**John:** We ³(      ) (      ) leave in 30 minutes. Will you be ready?

**Karen:** ⁴(      ) (      ). I'll be quick.

**John:** Did you check ⁵(      ) (      ) the flight is?

**Karen:** 7:30, but we're ⁶(      ) (      ) be at the gate at 7 o'clock.

**John:** We should ⁷(      ) (      ) the airport about 4:00.

**Karen:** Yes, then we can go shopping ⁸(      ) (      ) terminal.

---

### 🔍 Points to Dictate

ここでは会話の中で発生するいろいろな音の変化の聞き取りに挑戦してみましょう。空所の音変化は今まで練習してきた変化で構成されています。自分の耳がこれらの音変化に対応できるようになっていることを実感してください。

---

**✅ 頻出単語チェック！**    **Listening Section**

語句と意味を品詞に気をつけながら結びつけてみましょう。

1. board [v.] (   )     **a.** not the same as it was or as it was planned
2. line up (   )     **b.** about; not an exact number or amount
3. postpone (   )     **c.** to enter a plane, train, boat, or bus
4. approximately (   )     **d.** the place that you are going to
5. no longer (   )     **e.** to stand in a line to wait for something
6. take off [v.] (   )     **f.** trouble or problems
7. inconvenience (   )     **g.** to leave the ground and start flying
8. destination (   )     **h.** to change the time of something (e.g., a meeting) to later

## PART 1 　写真描写問題  2-62,63

*Check Point!* 　複数の人物の動作や物の状態について述べるケースを見てみましょう。
People are lining up at the door.

それぞれの写真について、4つの説明文の中から最も適切なものを1つずつ選びましょう。

1.

Ⓐ Ⓑ Ⓒ Ⓓ

2.

Ⓐ Ⓑ Ⓒ Ⓓ

## PART 2 　応答問題  2-64-68

*Check Point!* 　Have が文頭だと出来事の完了、Be 動詞だと主語の状態を尋ねます。
Have you already reserved a hotel?

それぞれの設問の応答として最も適切なものを1つずつ選びましょう。

**3.** Mark your answer on your answer sheet. 　　　　Ⓐ Ⓑ Ⓒ

**4.** Mark your answer on your answer sheet. 　　　　Ⓐ Ⓑ Ⓒ

**5.** Mark your answer on your answer sheet. 　　　　Ⓐ Ⓑ Ⓒ

**6.** Mark your answer on your answer sheet. 　　　　Ⓐ Ⓑ Ⓒ

**7.** Mark your answer on your answer sheet. 　　　　Ⓐ Ⓑ Ⓒ

**Check Point!**　話し手の一方が抱えている問題を聞き取りましょう。
What is the man's problem?

会話についての設問に対し、最も適切なものを 1 つずつ選びましょう。

**8.** What is the man's problem?
(A) He thinks that he is lost.
(B) He is late to meet someone.
(C) He is not feeling well.
(D) He has an old map.

**9.** Why is the man surprised?
(A) The station is far away.
(B) He walked past the station.
(C) He's on the wrong street.
(D) The station has moved.

**10.** Look at the graphic. Which building is the station?
(A) Building 1
(B) Building 2
(C) Building 3
(D) Building 4

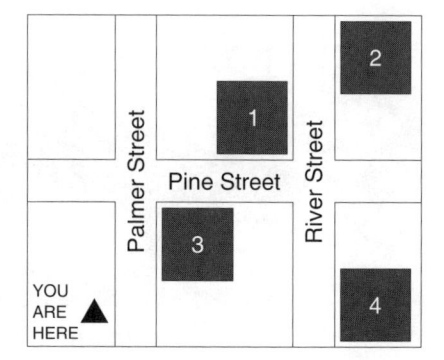

**PART 4** 説明文問題　　　　　　　　　　　　　　　　　　🔊 2-71,72

**Check Point!**　機内アナウンスで何が知らされているのか大きく捉えましょう。
According to the speaker, what caused the delay?

説明文についての設問に対し、最も適切なものを 1 つずつ選びましょう。

**11.** Look at the graphic. When was the flight supposed to leave?
(A) 11:35
(B) 11:45
(C) 11:50
(D) 12:00

**12.** According to the speaker, what caused the delay?
(A) Bad weather
(B) Technical problems
(C) Late staff
(D) Passenger illness

**13.** What does the speaker recommend?
(A) Going to the gate 45 minutes early
(B) Getting ready for take off
(C) Going to the convenience store
(D) Looking at the departure boards

| Flight Time | Flight | Destination | Gate |
|---|---|---|---|
| 11:35 | TR 486 | Vancouver | 15 |
| 11:45 | DR 561 | Montreal | 63 |
| 11:50 | DR 645 | Ottawa | 45 |
| 12:00 | TR 456 | Toronto | 53 |

##  Grammar Review 前置詞と接続詞

■**前置詞と接続詞**というテーマでは注意したい点が２つあります。

1．同じ意味でありながら**前置詞**と**接続詞**では用法が異なります。例えば during（前置詞）と while（接続詞）は「〜の間」という意味ですが、We enjoyed some delicious meals **during** our stay in Kyoto.（京都滞在<u>の間</u>美味しい料理を楽しんだ）。We enjoyed the beautiful sunset **while** we were sitting on the beach.（ビーチに座って<u>いる間</u>夕日を楽しんだ）となります。

2．before（〜の前）、after（〜の後）、since（〜以来）、as（〜として）など同じ語が前置詞と接続詞の両方に使われる場合には注意が必要です。前置詞なら I will call you **before** the flight.（フライトの前に電話します）で接続詞なら I will call you **before** I board the plane.（搭乗前に電話します）となります。

▶**前置詞と接続詞の見分け方**は、上の例でもわかるように、<u>前置詞の後ろには名詞（句）</u>が、<u>接続詞の後ろには主語＋動詞の節</u>が続くということを覚えておきましょう。

---

《例題》各空所に入れるべき最も適切な語を１つ選んで、その記号を答えなさい。

**1.** We will go shopping ------- the sightseeing tour.
　　(A) despite　　(B) after　　(C) unless　　(D) since

**2.** I took a taxi ------- the weather was bad.
　　(A) because　　(B) therefore　　(C) yet　　(D) unless

---

## Reading Section

### ✔ 頻出単語チェック！ Reading Section

語句と意味を品詞に気をつけながら結びつけてみましょう。

**1.** on time (　　)
**2.** serve [v.] (　　)
**3.** welcome (　　)
**4.** construction (　　)
**5.** journey [n.] (　　)
**6.** maintenance work (　　)
**7.** instead of (　　)
**8.** attach (　　)

**a.** work done to make sure that something continues to work well
**b.** a flight, train ride, bus ride, etc. from one place to another
**c.** changing this thing for another thing
**d.** to include a document in an e-mail
**e.** making things such as buildings, roads, and bridges
**f.** happening at the planned time; not late
**g.** to greet visitors and thank them for coming
**h.** to give food or drink to people

**Check Point!**  文法問題：前置詞と接続詞　語彙問題：動詞
前置詞の後ろは名詞で接続詞の後ろは節が続きます。

それぞれの空所に入れるのに最も適切なものを1つずつ選びましょう。

**14.** We were able to do some sightseeing ------- we were in Rome.
(A) also
(B) during
(C) therefore
(D) while           Ⓐ Ⓑ Ⓒ Ⓓ

**15.** We had lunch at a French restaurant ------- we visited the art museum.
(A) after
(B) during
(C) besides
(D) since           Ⓐ Ⓑ Ⓒ Ⓓ

**16.** ------- the bad weather, the train was on time and the journey was smooth.
(A) Although
(B) Because
(C) Despite
(D) However           Ⓐ Ⓑ Ⓒ Ⓓ

**17.** Please ------- for a taxi to take me to the airport at 6:00 A.M. tomorrow.
(A) arrange
(B) arrive
(C) assist
(D) accept           Ⓐ Ⓑ Ⓒ Ⓓ

**18.** We need to get to the train station before the last train -------.
(A) parks
(B) waits
(C) drives
(D) departs           Ⓐ Ⓑ Ⓒ Ⓓ

## PART 6 長文穴埋め問題

手紙　語彙問題：動詞、句動詞
文挿入問題：書き手が勧めている内容と合うものを選びましょう。

それぞれの空所に入れるのに最も適切なものを１つずつ選びましょう。

---

Seaview Hotel

375 Ocean Drive

Palm Beach

Miami

FL 33402


Dear Ms. Kawasaki,


Thank you for booking with us.


I am writing to confirm your reservation. We have reserved a double room for you from September 15 to September 22. ------- **19.** This will be served in the dining room on the first floor.


We also ------- **20.** a free bus between the airport and our hotel. Our bus will be waiting outside the main doors at the airport. It is very easy to find: It is a yellow bus and it has the name of our hotel on the side.


We look forward ------- **21.** your stay. Please ask if you have any questions.


Sincerely,


Jennifer Sanderson

Hotel Manager

---

**19.** (A) All our rooms come with televisions and coffee machines.
(B) Our staff are looking forward to welcoming you to our hotel.
(C) Your booking includes a free breakfast each morning.
(D) As you asked, we have reserved a room with a view of the beach.

**20.** (A) include
(B) provide
(C) deliver
(D) give

**21.** (A) for
(B) of
(C) on
(D) to

## PART 7　読解問題

文章を読んで、それぞれの設問の答えとして最も適切なものを1つずつ選びましょう。

| Schedule for Trip to Howard's Foods | |
|---|---|
| **7:30 A.M.** | Subway to Main Street |
| **8:05 A.M.** | Train from Main Street to West Trenton |
| **9:30 A.M.** | Taxi to Howard's Foods office |
| **9:45 A.M.** | Meeting with John Edwards and Jacqueline Petit to discuss building their new factory |
| **12:00 P.M.** | Taxi to West Trenton |
| **12:30 P.M.** | Train from West Trenton to Main Street |
| **1:55 P.M.** | Subway to office |

 **E-MAIL**

| To: | Ian Sanderson <i.sanderson@moore-construction.com> |
| From: | Mary Rogers <m.rogers@moore-construction.com> |
| Date: | October 12 |
| Subject: | Information about your journey tomorrow |

Dear Ian,

I hope you are well.

I am writing to suggest a change to your travel plans tomorrow because of maintenance work between Main Street Station and West Trenton Station.

This maintenance work is due to take place tomorrow morning. No trains will run at this time.

I recommend that you take the subway to Central Station instead of Main Street Station. You can catch another train from there to West Trenton. You will need to leave a little earlier in the morning. I suggest getting the 7:35 A.M. train from Central Station. I've attached the train schedule for you.

Please ask if you need any help.

Kind regards,

Mary Rogers

| TRAINS TO WEST TRENTON | | |
|---|---|---|
| Central Station | Main Street Station | West Trenton Station |
| Dep. | Dep. | Arr. |
| 07:35 | - | 09:35 |
| - | 07:35 | 09:00 |
| 07:55 | - | 09:55 |
| - | 08:05 | 09:30 |

22. What type of business does Ms. Rogers most likely work for?
    (A) A transportation company
    (B) A construction company
    (C) A food company
    (D) A travel agency

23. Why did Ms. Rogers contact her coworker?
    (A) To provide a schedule for a trip
    (B) To announce a new project
    (C) To reserve some train tickets
    (D) To recommend a change in plans

24. In the e-mail, the word "due" in paragraph 3, line 1, is closest in meaning to
    (A) caused
    (B) delayed
    (C) expected
    (D) accepted

25. What time will Mr. Sanderson likely arrive at West Trenton Station?
    (A) 09:00
    (B) 09:30
    (C) 09:35
    (D) 09:55

# UNIT

## 14

# Housing / Corporate Property

**Warm up** | **Dictation Practice**  2-73

それぞれの空所に入る語を、音声を聞いて書き入れてみましょう。

Hi, this is Mike ¹( ) ( ) Housing Team.
I'm ²( ) ( ) let you know that the new community center
³( ) ( ) open.
You can ⁴( ) ( ) and take a look anytime
⁵( ) ( ).
We're sure you'll ⁶( ) ( ) useful.
If you have ⁷( ) ( ), we'd ⁸( )
( ) hear them.
Thanks!

> **Points to Dictate**
>
> ここでは電話メッセージの中で発生するいろいろな音の変化の聞き取りに
> 挑戦してみましょう。空所の音変化は今まで練習してきた変化で構成され
> ています。自分の耳がこれらの音変化に対応できるようになっていること
> を実感してください。

**✓ 頻出単語チェック！** **Listening Section**

語句と意味を品詞に気をつけながら結びつけてみましょう。

1. afford (    )
2. manage (    )
3. take care of (    )
4. forecast [n.] (    )
5. interior (    )
6. update [v.] (    )
7. on schedule (    )
8. stage [n.] (    )

a. what experts think will happen in the future (usually about the weather)
b. the inside of something (e.g., a building)
c. to deal with something; to do a task
d. happening at the time it was planned
e. to control and lead a company or business
f. to be able to buy or pay for something
g. a step in a process
h. to give the latest information about something

102

# Listening Section

## PART 1　写真描写問題

 2-74,75

**Check Point!** 物が主語となり、その状態について述べるケースを見てみましょう。
Some clothes are in the closet.

それぞれの写真について、4つの説明文の中から最も適切なものを1つずつ選びましょう。

**1.**

(A) (B) (C) (D)

**2.**

(A) (B) (C) (D)

## PART 2　応答問題

 2-76-80

**Check Point!** 付加疑問文は「確認や同意」を求めます。
You moved to a new apartment, didn't you?

それぞれの設問の応答として最も適切なものを1つずつ選びましょう。

**3.** Mark your answer on your answer sheet.　(A) (B) (C)

**4.** Mark your answer on your answer sheet.　(A) (B) (C)

**5.** Mark your answer on your answer sheet.　(A) (B) (C)

**6.** Mark your answer on your answer sheet.　(A) (B) (C)

**7.** Mark your answer on your answer sheet.　(A) (B) (C)

> ***Check Point!*** 話し手の一方が誰なのか聞き取りましょう。
> Who most likely is the man?

会話についての設問に対し、最も適切なものを1つずつ選びましょう。

**8.** Who most likely is the man?
(A) A painter
(B) A gardener
(C) An interior designer
(D) A mechanic

**9.** Look at the graphic. When will the man come back?
(A) Monday
(B) Wednesday
(C) Thursday
(D) Friday

**10.** How can the man contact the woman?
(A) By phone
(B) By e-mail
(C) By visiting
(D) By mail

| Day | Weather |
|---|---|
| Monday | ☀ |
| Tuesday | ☔ |
| Wednesday | 🌤 |
| Thursday | ☔ |
| Friday | ☀ |

**PART 4**　説明文問題　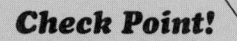　2-83,84

> ***Check Point!*** 話し手はどのような職業に就いているか聞き取りましょう。
> What kind of business does the speaker work for?

説明文についての設問に対し、最も適切なものを1つずつ選びましょう。

**11.** What kind of business does the speaker work for?
(A) A fashion company
(B) A computer company
(C) A travel company
(D) A housing company

**12.** What is the purpose of the call?
(A) To report progress
(B) To apologize for a delay
(C) To confirm a decision
(D) To change the schedule

**13.** Look at the graphic. On what day would the speaker like to meet?
(A) May 16
(B) May 30
(C) June 16
(D) June 30

| Stage | Start date |
|---|---|
| Kitchen and bathroom | May 16 |
| Living room | May 30 |
| Bedroom | June 16 |
| Dining room | June 30 |

## 📝 **Grammar Review** 比較

■**比較級には3種類**あります。**比較級、最上級、原級**です。

▶**比較級**：「AはBより〜だ」のように2つの物事を比較する際に使います。形容詞・副詞の語尾に -er を付けるか、形容詞・副詞が長い場合は -er の代わりに more を付け *more beautiful* とします。他に interesting や comfortable などがあります。Our new office building is **more comfortable** *than* our previous one.（我々の新しいオフィスビルは以前のものより快適だ）。注目は than で、比較級である目安の語です。

▶**最上級**：「Aは最も〜だ」と比較する対象の中で最上位を表す際に使われます。the＋形容詞・副詞の語尾に -est を付けるか、形容詞・副詞が長い場合は most を使い *most beautiful* とします。This apartment building is *the* **tallest** in the city.（このアパートは市内で最も高い）。

▶**原級**：「〜において同じだ」のように同等の物事を「as 原級 as」の形で表現するのが基本です。This apartment is *as* **large** *as* the one we saw yesterday.（昨日見たのと同じ大きさだ）

《例題》各空所に入れるべき最も適切な語句を1つ選んで、その記号を答えなさい。

1. This neighborhood is as ------- as our previous one.
   (A) quiet      (B) quieter      (C) quietest      (D) most quiet

2. The meeting room on the top floor has the ------- view in the building.
   (A) good      (B) better      (C) best      (D) much better

## Reading Section

### ✅ 頻出単語チェック！ Reading Section

語句と意味を品詞に気をつけながら結びつけてみましょう。

1. current [adj.] (      )
2. ceiling (      )
3. immediately (      )
4. hesitate (      )
5. on behalf of (      )
6. resident [n.] (      )
7. parking lot (      )
8. parking spot (      )

a. an area of land where cars can park
b. being used on owned now
c. an area for one car to park
d. to be slow to say something because you feel shy or uncertain
e. a person who lives in a particular area or building
f. right now, without waiting
g. speaking on doing something for a group of people
h. the top part of a room (on the inside)

それぞれの空所に入れるのに最も適切なものを1つずつ選びましょう。

**14.** Our current office is not as ------- as the office that we used before.
(A) big
(B) bigger
(C) biggest
(D) much bigger

Ⓐ Ⓑ Ⓒ Ⓓ

**15.** The ceiling in our new apartment is ------- than in our old one.
(A) high
(B) higher
(C) highest
(D) highly

Ⓐ Ⓑ Ⓒ Ⓓ

**16.** The First Bank is the ------- to walk to from our office.
(A) more easily
(B) easy
(C) most easily
(D) easiest

Ⓐ Ⓑ Ⓒ Ⓓ

**17.** The manager asked the building owner to fix the problem with the water -------.
(A) immediately
(B) slightly
(C) gradually
(D) extremely

Ⓐ Ⓑ Ⓒ Ⓓ

**18.** Although this apartment is near the station, it's ------- cheap compared to similar ones.
(A) highly
(B) exactly
(C) relatively
(D) specially

Ⓐ Ⓑ Ⓒ Ⓓ

*Check Point!*  手紙　語彙問題：数量表現、動詞
文挿入問題：書き手が勧めている内容と合うものを選びましょう。

それぞれの空所に入れるのに最も適切なものを１つずつ選びましょう。

---

Sun City Apartments

123 Market Street

Sun City

LA 90210


Dear Ms. Partridge,


It was a pleasure to meet you on Tuesday.


I am writing to ask if you have any questions about the apartments that you saw
-------- days ago. If you need more information about them, please ask.
**19.**


I should also tell you that some other people are interested in buying the
apartment on Station Road. -------- So, if you are interested in this apartment, I
**20.**
suggest you contact me quickly.


If you would like to -------- some more apartments, please do not hesitate to
**21.**
contact me. I will be very pleased to arrange some more visits.


Best regards,


Anita Jerome

Real Estate Agent

---

**19.** (A) few
(B) a few
(C) little
(D) a little

**20.** (A) I think this apartment will be sold soon.
(B) I am sure that we can sell this for you.
(C) I am very sorry that it was already sold.
(D) Thank you very much for your interest.

**21.** (A) go
(B) buy
(C) interview
(D) see

## PART 7　読解問題

文章を読んで、それぞれの設問の答えとして最も適切なものを１つずつ選びましょう。

Jasmine Potter
Apartment 4
Parkside Apartment Building
Forest Road
Meadowville
VR 05058

Dear Mr. Morris,

On behalf of the residents group, I want to welcome you to your new apartment. The residents group works together to look after the building. For example, a few years ago, we hired someone to paint the outside of the building.

We would love to meet you at our next monthly residents group meeting on September 8. If you would like to come, please send an e-mail to me: jasmine.potter@residents-email.com

I have also included a map of the parking lot with this letter. This shows which parking spots are for residents and which can be used by guests. Your parking spot is 7. I have also included instructions for how to reserve guest parking spots.

If you have any questions, feel free to contact me.

Jasmine Potter
President of the Residents Group

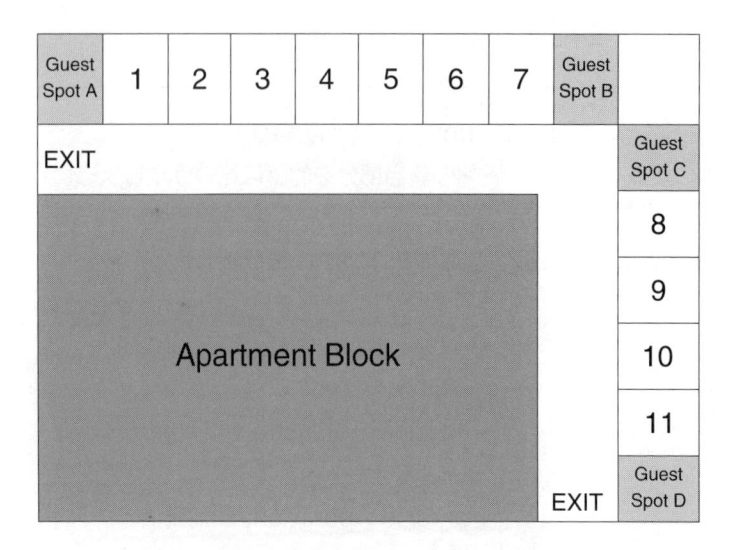

**Instructions for Reserving Guest Parking Spots**

1. Please access the parking reservation Web site.

2. Click the date on the calendar when your guests will visit. You will see which guest parking spots are available.

3. Click the spot you want and then click the 'reserve' button. Please do not reserve a spot for more than three days at a time. If you need to do this, please e-mail Ms. Potter.

If you need any help with this Web site, please contact Ms. Potter.

**22.** What is the main purpose of the letter?
(A) To introduce the residents group
(B) To explain some maintenance work
(C) To ask a question about parking
(D) To remind someone of the parking rules

**23.** In the letter, what is indicated about the residents group?
(A) They have a meeting every week.
(B) They painted the building this year.
(C) They control the parking spots.
(D) They do not have a leader.

**24.** What is true about Mr. Morris's parking spot?
(A) It's in the center of a row.
(B) It's next to a guest parking spot.
(C) It's parking spot 10.
(D) It's near an exit to the parking lot.

**25.** According to the instructions, what must residents do to reserve a guest spot for a week?
(A) Reserve it through the Web site
(B) Ask at a residents meeting
(C) Fill out a request form online
(D) Send an e-mail to Ms. Potter

# TOEIC 必須複合名詞 100

|  | |  |  |
|---|---|---|---|
| 1 | ☐ | accounting department | 経理部 |
| 2 | ☐ | accounting firm | 会計事務所 |
| 3 | ☐ | additional cost | 追加費用 |
| 4 | ☐ | admission fee | 入場料 |
| 5 | ☐ | advertising agency | 広告代理店 |
| 6 | ☐ | advertising department | 宣伝部 |
| 7 | ☐ | amusement park | 遊園地 |
| 8 | ☐ | annual event | 年間行事 |
| 9 | ☐ | annual meeting | 年次会合 |
| 10 | ☐ | application form | 申込書 |
| 11 | ☐ | arrival time | 到着時刻 |
| 12 | ☐ | assembly line | 組立ライン |
| 13 | ☐ | board meeting | 取締役会議 |
| 14 | ☐ | boarding pass | 搭乗券 |
| 15 | ☐ | branch manager | 支店長 |
| 16 | ☐ | branch office | 支店 |
| 17 | ☐ | bulletin board | 掲示板 |
| 18 | ☐ | business days | 営業日 |
| 19 | ☐ | business hours | 業務「営業」時間 |
| 20 | ☐ | business owner | 事業主 |
| 21 | ☐ | cash register | レジ |
| 22 | ☐ | catering service | ケータリングサービス |
| 23 | ☐ | CEO | 最高経営責任者 |
| 24 | ☐ | city hall | 市役所 |
| 25 | ☐ | conference call | 電話会議 |
| 26 | ☐ | construction worker | 建設作業員 |
| 27 | ☐ | contact information | 連絡先情報 |
| 28 | ☐ | company brochure | 会社案内 |
| 29 | ☐ | construction site | 工事現場 |
| 30 | ☐ | cost saving | コスト節約 |
| 31 | ☐ | cover letter | カバーレター |
| 32 | ☐ | customer service | カスタマーサービス |
| 33 | ☐ | delivery date | 配達日 |
| 34 | ☐ | departure time | 出発時刻 |
| 35 | ☐ | discount coupon | 割引券 |
| 36 | ☐ | due date | 提出期限 |
| 37 | ☐ | eating habits | 食習慣 |
| 38 | ☐ | educational program | 教育番組 |
| 39 | ☐ | electronic device | 電子機器 |
| 40 | ☐ | entry fee | 参加費 |
| 41 | ☐ | executive director | 事務局長 |
| 42 | ☐ | expiration date | 有効期限 |
| 43 | ☐ | extra charge | 追加料金 |
| 44 | ☐ | extra work | 超過勤務 |
| 45 | ☐ | fitting room | 試着室 |
| 46 | ☐ | flight attendant | 客室乗務員 |
| 47 | ☐ | further information | 詳細 |
| 48 | ☐ | general manager | 部長 |
| 49 | ☐ | great success | 大成功 |
| 50 | ☐ | healthy food | 健康食品 |

| 51 | ☐ | home appliances | 家電製品 |
|---|---|---|---|
| 52 | ☐ | human resources | 人事部 |
| 53 | ☐ | identification badge | 身分証明証 |
| 54 | ☐ | information technology | 情報技術 |
| 55 | ☐ | job interview | 採用面接 |
| 56 | ☐ | job offer | 仕事の口 |
| 57 | ☐ | local news | ローカルニュース |
| 58 | ☐ | medical history | 病歴 |
| 59 | ☐ | medical treatment | 医療 |
| 60 | ☐ | membership fee | 会費 |
| 61 | ☐ | newspaper article | 新聞記事 |
| 62 | ☐ | office equipment | オフィス機器 |
| 63 | ☐ | office supply | 事務用品 |
| 64 | ☐ | opening ceremony | 開会式 |
| 65 | ☐ | online form | オンライン・フォーム |
| 66 | ☐ | plane ticket | 航空券 |
| 67 | ☐ | press conference | 記者会見 |
| 68 | ☐ | price list | 価格表 |
| 69 | ☐ | price tag | 値札 |
| 70 | ☐ | public relations | 広報 |
| 71 | ☐ | public transportation | 公共交通機関 |
| 72 | ☐ | registration fee | 登録料 |
| 73 | ☐ | regular price | 通常価格 |
| 74 | ☐ | residential area | 住宅街 |
| 75 | ☐ | retail store | 小売店 |
| 76 | ☐ | return ticket | 帰りのチケット |
| 77 | ☐ | road construction | 道路工事 |
| 78 | ☐ | safety inspection | 安全検査 |
| 79 | ☐ | sales department | 営業部 |
| 80 | ☐ | sales increase | 売り上げ増 |
| 81 | ☐ | sales manager | 営業 [ 販売 ] 部長 |
| 82 | ☐ | sales promotion | 販売促進活動 |
| 83 | ☐ | sales representative | 販売員 |
| 84 | ☐ | savings account | 普通預金口座 |
| 85 | ☐ | security guard | 警備員 |
| 86 | ☐ | shipping address | 配送先住所 |
| 87 | ☐ | shopping cart | ショッピングカート |
| 88 | ☐ | social media | ソーシャルメディア |
| 89 | ☐ | store owner | 店主 |
| 90 | ☐ | technical support | テクニカルサポート |
| 91 | ☐ | text message | テキストメッセージ |
| 92 | ☐ | traffic report | 交通情報 |
| 93 | ☐ | training manual | トレーニングマニュアル |
| 94 | ☐ | training session | 研修会 |
| 95 | ☐ | travel agent | 旅行代理店 |
| 96 | ☐ | travel expense | 旅費 |
| 97 | ☐ | user's manual | 取扱説明書 |
| 98 | ☐ | vice president | 副社長 |
| 99 | ☐ | work experience | 実務経験 |
| 100 | ☐ | work hours | 労働「勤務」時間 |

# TOEIC 重要熟語 100

| | | 見出し語 | 例文 |
|---|---|---|---|
| 1 | ☐ | according to | According to the schedule, the meeting starts at 11 A.M. |
| 2 | ☐ | account for | She needs to account for all the project costs. |
| 3 | ☐ | ahead of time | We could finished the report ahead of time. |
| 4 | ☐ | along with | He came along with his coworker to the training session. |
| 5 | ☐ | around the clock | The store is open around the clock every day. |
| 6 | ☐ | as a result of | As a result of the heavy rain, the event was canceled. |
| 7 | ☐ | as far as | As far as I know, it's correct. |
| 8 | ☐ | as long as | You can take a vacation as long as you finish this work. |
| 9 | ☐ | as of | As of tomorrow, the new rules will start. |
| 10 | ☐ | as soon as | Please call me as soon as you arrive at the office. |
| 11 | ☐ | A as well as B | He speaks French as well as English. |
| 12 | ☐ | at least | We need at least five more chairs. |
| 13 | ☐ | at the moment | She is out at the moment. |
| 14 | ☐ | be about to do | I was about to call you. |
| 15 | ☐ | be afraid of | She is afraid of heights. |
| 16 | ☐ | be aware of | Are you aware of the risks? |
| 17 | ☐ | be capable of | She is capable of leading the team. |
| 18 | ☐ | be different from | This is different from what I expected. |
| 19 | ☐ | be familiar with | Are you familiar with this software? |
| 20 | ☐ | be famous for | Paris is famous for its various art museums. |
| 21 | ☐ | be full of | The box is full of books. |
| 22 | ☐ | be headed for | He is headed for the conference room. |
| 23 | ☐ | be in charge of | She is in charge of the European market. |
| 24 | ☐ | be interested in | Are you interested in this job? |
| 25 | ☐ | be made of | The table is made of wood. |
| 26 | ☐ | be responsible for | He is responsible for the business travel schedule. |
| 27 | ☐ | be satisfied with | She is satisfied with the results. |
| 28 | ☐ | be similar to | This is similar to my first car. |
| 29 | ☐ | because of | The picnic was canceled because of the bad weather. |
| 30 | ☐ | behind schedule | The train is behind schedule by five minutes. |
| 31 | ☐ | bound for | This flight is bound for New York. |
| 32 | ☐ | by means of | They communicated by means of e-mails. |
| 33 | ☐ | by mistake | I deleted an important email by mistake. |
| 34 | ☐ | by the time | By the time I arrived, he had left. |
| 35 | ☐ | call off | They called off the conference because of the typhoon. |

| 意味 | 訳 |
|---|---|
| ～によれば | スケジュールによると、会議は午前11時に始まります。 |
| ～の説明責任を負う | 彼女はプロジェクトの全ての費用を説明する必要があります。 |
| ～決められた時間より前に | その報告書を予定より早く書き上げることができました。 |
| ～と一緒に | 彼は同僚と一緒に研修に来ました。 |
| まる一日中 | その店は毎日24時間営業しています。 |
| ～の結果として | 豪雨で、そのイベントは中止されました。 |
| ～する限り | 私の知る限り、それは正しいです。 |
| ～である限り | この仕事を完了させれば、休暇を取ることができます。 |
| ～の時点で | 明日の時点で新しいルールが始まります。 |
| ～するとすぐに | 会社に着いたらすぐに私に電話してください。 |
| BだけでなくAも | 彼は英語だけでなくフランス語も話します。 |
| 少なくとも | 私たちは少なくともあと5つの椅子が必要です。 |
| 今のところ | 彼女は今出かけています。 |
| ～しようとしている | ちょうどあなたに電話しようとしていました。 |
| ～を恐れる | 彼女は高いところが苦手です。 |
| ～に気づいている | あなたはそのリスクに気づいていますか？ |
| ～する能力がある | 彼女にはチームをリードする能力があります。 |
| ～と異なる | これは私が予想していたものとは違います。 |
| ～に精通している | あなたはこのソフトウェアに詳しいですか？ |
| ～で有名である | パリはさまざまな美術館で有名です。 |
| ～でいっぱいである | その箱は本でいっぱいです。 |
| ～に向かって進む | 彼は会議室に向かっています。 |
| ～を担当している | 彼女は欧州マーケットを担当しています。 |
| ～に興味がある | あなたはこの仕事に興味がありますか？ |
| ～でできている | そのテーブルは木でできています。 |
| ～に責任がある | 彼は出張のスケジュールを担当しています。 |
| ～に満足している | 彼女は結果に満足しています。 |
| ～と似ている | これは私の最初の車に似ています。 |
| ～のために | 悪天候のため、ピクニックがキャンセルされました。 |
| 予定に遅れて | 列車が5分遅れています。 |
| ～行きの | このフライトはニューヨーク行きです。 |
| ～によって | 彼らはメールを使って連絡を取りました。 |
| 誤って | 私は間違って重要なメールを削除しました。 |
| ～時までに | 私が到着した時には、彼はもう出発していました。 |
| ～を中止する | 彼らは台風のため学会を中止しました。 |

| | | 見出し語 | 例文 |
|---|---|---|---|
| 36 | ☐ | check in | Please check in at the front desk when you arrive. |
| 37 | ☐ | come up with | She came up with a good idea. |
| 38 | ☐ | concentrate on | It's hard to concentrate on reading in this noise. |
| 39 | ☐ | deal with | He deals with problems in the office. |
| 40 | ☐ | divide A into B | Please divide the class into two groups. |
| 41 | ☐ | due to | The flight was delayed due to fog. |
| 42 | ☐ | even though | He passed the test even though it was hard. |
| 43 | ☐ | except for | Everyone except for John is here. |
| 44 | ☐ | fill out | Please fill out this form before the interview. |
| 45 | ☐ | focus on | He is trying to focus on the lecture. |
| 46 | ☐ | for instance | I like fruit, for instance, apples and oranges. |
| 47 | ☐ | for reference | You can use this chart for reference. |
| 48 | ☐ | for the purpose of | The information desk is for the purpose of helping visitors. |
| 49 | ☐ | free of charge | Parking is free of charge after 6 P.M. |
| 50 | ☐ | get along with | She gets along with everyone in the office. |
| 51 | ☐ | get in touch with | How can I get in touch with you? |
| 52 | ☐ | go on | Let's go on to the next topic. |
| 53 | ☐ | go over | Can we go over the schedule once more? |
| 54 | ☐ | hang up | She hung up the phone quickly after the call. |
| 55 | ☐ | in addition to | In addition to snow, there was strong wind. |
| 56 | ☐ | in case of | In case of fire, use the stairs. |
| 57 | ☐ | in comparison with | In comparison with Tokyo, Sydney is smaller. |
| 58 | ☐ | in fact | In fact, the weather was better than we thought. |
| 59 | ☐ | inform A of B | The teacher informed the students of the test date. |
| 60 | ☐ | in order to | He saved money in order to buy a new car. |
| 61 | ☐ | in spite of | She went to work in spite of feeling sick. |
| 62 | ☐ | in the middle of | She was in the middle of a phone call. |
| 63 | ☐ | in the process of | Her first book was in the process of being published. |
| 64 | ☐ | in time | He finished his work just in time. |
| 65 | ☐ | instead of | We took the bus instead of a taxi. |
| 66 | ☐ | keep in mind | The manager asked us to keep in mind the deadline. |
| 67 | ☐ | keep in touch | Let's keep in touch after you move. |
| 68 | ☐ | look forward to | I look forward to seeing you. |
| 69 | ☐ | look into | We need to look into this problem right away. |
| 70 | ☐ | make a decision | She made a decision to study abroad. |

| 意味 | 訳 |
|---|---|
| チェックインする | 到着したらフロントでチェックインしてください。 |
| 〜を思いつく | 彼女は良いアイデアを思いつきました。 |
| 〜に集中する | この騒音では読書に集中するのが難しいです。 |
| 〜に対処する | 彼はオフィス内の問題に対応しています。 |
| A を B に分ける | クラスを 2 つのグループに分けてください。 |
| 〜のために | フライトは霧のため遅れました。 |
| 〜にもかかわらず | 難しかったけれども、彼はテストに合格しました。 |
| 〜を除いて | ジョンを除いて全員がここにいます。 |
| 〜に書き込みをする | 面接の前にこの用紙に記入してください。 |
| 〜に集中する | 彼は講義に集中しようとしています。 |
| 例えば | 私は例えば、リンゴやオレンジといった果物が好きです。 |
| 参考まで | この図を参考に使うことができます。 |
| 〜のために | インフォメーションデスクは訪問者を助けるためのものです。 |
| 無料で | 駐車場は午後 6 時以降無料です。 |
| 〜とうまくやっていく | 彼女はオフィスの皆とうまくやっています。 |
| 〜と連絡を取る | あなたにどうやって連絡を取ればいいですか？ |
| 続ける | 次の話題に進みましょう。 |
| 〜を見直す | もう一度スケジュールを確認できますか？ |
| （電話を）切る | 彼女は通話後、すぐに電話を切りました。 |
| 〜に加えて | 雪に加えて、強い風もありました。 |
| 〜の場合に | 火事の場合は、階段を使ってください。 |
| 〜と比べて | 東京と比べて、シドニーは小さいです。 |
| 実際には | 実際、天気は私たちが思っていたよりも良かったです。 |
| A に B を知らせる | 先生は生徒たちに試験の日程を知らせました。 |
| 〜するために | 彼は新しい車を買うためにお金を貯めました。 |
| 〜にもかかわらず | 彼女は体調が悪いにもかかわらず仕事に行きました。 |
| 〜の真ん中に | 彼女は電話の最中でした。 |
| 〜の過程で | 彼女の最初の本は出版される過程にありました。 |
| 間に合って | 彼はちょうど間に合って仕事を終えました。 |
| 〜の代わりに | 私たちはタクシーの代わりにバスに乗りました。 |
| 〜を心に留める | マネージャーは締め切りを覚えておくように言いました。 |
| 連絡を取り続ける | 引っ越した後も連絡を取り続けましょう。 |
| 〜を楽しみにする | お会いするのを楽しみにしています。 |
| 〜を調べる | 私たちはこの問題をすぐに調査する必要があります。 |
| 決定する | 彼女は留学する決断をしました。 |

| | | 見出し語 | 例文 |
|---|---|---|---|
| 71 | ☐ | make a difference | Small changes can make a big difference. |
| 72 | ☐ | make sure | Please make sure the door is locked. |
| 73 | ☐ | no longer | He no longer works at this company. |
| 74 | ☐ | on behalf of | He signed the document on behalf of the company. |
| 75 | ☐ | on time | The meeting started on time. |
| 76 | ☐ | pay attention to | It's important to pay attention to your health. |
| 77 | ☐ | pick up | I will pick up my friend at the station. |
| 78 | ☐ | prior to | He reviewed the report prior to the meeting. |
| 79 | ☐ | put off | They put off the game because the field was too wet. |
| 80 | ☐ | put up with | We have to put up with the heavy traffic every morning. |
| 81 | ☐ | refer to | Please refer to the manual for more information. |
| 82 | ☐ | relate to | These numbers relate to our sales. |
| 83 | ☐ | rely on | They rely on good weather for the event. |
| 84 | ☐ | result in | The new plan resulted in higher sales. |
| 85 | ☐ | run into | I ran into an old friend at the shopping center. |
| 86 | ☐ | run out of | He ran out of gas on his way home. |
| 87 | ☐ | sign up | She signed up for the gym last week. |
| 88 | ☐ | so far | He has saved $100 so far. |
| 89 | ☐ | stop by | Please stop by my office after the meeting. |
| 90 | ☐ | take advantage of | You should take advantage of this opportunity. |
| 91 | ☐ | take care of | Please take care of yourself while traveling. |
| 92 | ☐ | take part in | They are going to take part in the workshop. |
| 93 | ☐ | thanks to | Thanks to you, we finished the project on time. |
| 94 | ☐ | turn on | He turned on the computer to check his e-mail. |
| 95 | ☐ | under construction | The new office building is still under construction. |
| 96 | ☐ | up to | The final decision is up to the manager. |
| 97 | ☐ | used to | He used to work at this company. |
| 98 | ☐ | without doubt | Without doubt, this book will be a bestseller. |
| 99 | ☐ | without notice | The service was stopped without notice. |
| 100 | ☐ | work out | I hope everything works out in the end. |

| 意味 | 訳 |
| --- | --- |
| 違いを生む | 小さな変化が大きな違いを生むことがあります。 |
| 〜を確認する | ドアが施錠されていることを確認してください。 |
| もはや〜でない | 彼はもうこの会社で働いていません。 |
| 〜を代表して | 彼は会社を代表して書類に署名しました。 |
| 時間通りに | 会議は時間通りに始まりました。 |
| 〜に注意を払う | 健康に注意を払うことは大切です。 |
| 〜を迎えに行く | 駅に友達を迎えに行きます。 |
| 〜より前に | 彼は会議の前にレポートを見直しました。 |
| 〜を延期する | フィールドが濡れすぎていたので、試合を延期しました。 |
| 〜に耐える | 私たちは毎朝、渋滞に耐えなければなりません。 |
| 〜を参照する | 詳細についてはマニュアルを参照してください。 |
| 関連する | これらの数字は私たちの売上に関係しています。 |
| 〜に頼る | 彼らはイベントのために天気が良いことを頼りにしています。 |
| 〜の結果となる | 新しい計画が売上の増加をもたらしました。 |
| 〜に偶然出会う | ショッピングモールで昔の友達に偶然会いました。 |
| 〜を使い果たす | 彼は帰宅途中でガソリンがなくなりました。 |
| 登録を申し込む | 彼女は先週、ジムに登録しました。 |
| これまでのところ | 彼はこれまでに 100 ドル貯めました。 |
| 〜に立ち寄る | 会議の後、私のオフィスに立ち寄ってください。 |
| 〜を利用する | あなたはこの機会を活用するべきです。 |
| 〜の世話をする | 旅行中は自分の体に気をつけてください。 |
| 〜に参加する | 彼らはワークショップに参加する予定です。 |
| 〜のおかげで | あなたのおかげで、プロジェクトを時間通りに終えました。 |
| 〜をつける | 彼はメールを確認するためにコンピュータをつけました。 |
| 建設中 | 新しいオフィスビルはまだ建設中です。 |
| 〜次第で | 最終的な決定はマネージャー次第です。 |
| 以前は〜だった | 彼は以前、この会社で働いていました。 |
| 疑いもなく | 間違いなく、この本はベストセラーになるでしょう。 |
| 予告なしに | サービスは予告なしに停止されました。 |
| うまくいく | 最終的にすべてがうまくいくといいですね。 |

## TEXT PRODUCTION STAFF

| edited by | 編集 |
|---|---|
| Fumi Matsumoto | 松本　風見 |
| Mitsugu Shishido | 宍戸　貢 |

| cover design by | 表紙デザイン |
|---|---|
| Nobuyoshi Fujino | 藤野　伸芳 |

| text design by | 本文デザイン |
|---|---|
| Nobuyoshi Fujino | 藤野　伸芳 |

| English-language editing by | 英文校閲 |
|---|---|
| Matthew Millar | マシュー・ミラー |

## CD PRODUCTION STAFF

| narrated by | 吹き込み者 |
|---|---|
| Dominic Allen (AmE) | ドミニク・アレン (アメリカ英語) |
| Anya Floris (AmE) | アーニャ・フロレス（アメリカ英語） |
| Rachel Smith (BrE) | レイチェル・スミス（イギリス英語） |

# BEST PRACTICE FOR THE TOEIC® L&R TEST
# —Pre-Intermediate—

## TOEIC® L&R TESTへの総合アプローチ —Pre-Intermediate—

2025年1月20日　初版発行
2025年2月15日　第2刷発行

著　者　吉塚　弘
　　　　Graham Skerritt

発 行 者　佐野　英一郎

発 行 所　株式会社 成 美 堂
　　　　　〒101-0052　東京都千代田区神田小川町3-22
　　　　　TEL 03-3291-2261　FAX 03-3293-5490
　　　　　https://www.seibido.co.jp

印刷·製本　倉敷印刷株式会社

ISBN 978-4-7919-7313-2　　　　　　　　　　　Printed in Japan